THE GREAT APOSTASY

BY
JACK MICHAEL

Scripture quotations in this publication, unless otherwise indicated, are from, "The New King James Version. Copyright © 1979, 1980, 1982, Thomas Nelson Inc., Publishers."

"Scripture quotations marked (AMP) are from the Amplified Bible. Old Testament copyright © 1965, 1987 by the Zondervan Corporation. The Amplified New Testament copyright © 1958, 1987 by the Lockman Foundation. Used by permission."

"Scripture quotations marked (NIV) are taken from the HOLY BIBLE, New International Version, copyright © 1973, 1978, 1984, International Bible Society. Used by permission of Zondervan Bible Publishers."

Scripture quotations marked (KJV) are taken from the King James Version of the Bible.

Printed in the United States of America. All rights reserved under International Copyright Law. Contents and/or cover may not be reproduced in whole or in part in any form without the express written consent of the publisher.

THE GREAT APOSTASY
ISBN 0-9717827-1-7
Copyright © 2003 by Jack Michael

Published by
Jack Michael Outreach Ministries
P. O. Box 10688
Winston-Salem, NC 27108-0688

NOTE: Throughout this book, there are words or phrases enclosed in parenthesis within a quoted portion of scripture. Although these words and phrases are not an actual part of the scripture, they are, in fact, explanations or emphases derived from scriptural word studies.

TABLE OF CONTENTS

Preface	Page V
Introduction	Page VII
Apostasy Defined	Page 11
Once Saved, Always Saved?	Page 19
Secret Lives	Page 29
Shipwrecked Faith	Page 39
Forbidding to Marry	Page 53
Abstaining From Foods	Page 61
Comfort Zones	Page 73
Times And Seasons	Page 83
The End Times Church	Page 91
The Severity of Apostasy	Page 101
The Way Of Repentance	Page 109
Epilogue	Page 115

PREFACE

During March 2002, I was spending some personal time with the Lord. One morning, as I was walking along a deserted beach on the coast of North Carolina, and praying for the Lord's direction, the Holy Spirit spoke a strong, clear word to me...

WRITE A BOOK ON THE SUBJECT OF THE GREAT APOSTASY.

The Bible clearly informs us that prior to the return of the Lord Jesus Christ, there will be a time of falling away from the faith, also known as apostasy.

Of course, apostasy has been among us since the inception of the church. However, in 2 Thessalonians 2:1-3, the Apostle Paul warned about a specific time of apostasy in the End Times; thus, the title of this book: THE GREAT APOSTASY.

As I continued walking along the beach that chilly morning in March, I experienced a great urgency in my spirit. I believe the Lord impressed upon me that we have actually entered this grievous time in church history – the falling away from the faith prior to the return of the Lord Jesus Christ.

This book was perhaps the most difficult assignment to date for the writing ministry to which the Lord has called me. Apostasy is a very controversial subject.

I fervently prayed for God's clear direction the entire time I worked on the manuscript. The constant cry of my heart was: *"Heavenly Father, please help me to write the truth; please help me to be scripturally accurate!"*

I trust that God has done as he promised in John 16:13:

"However, when He, the Spirit of truth, has come, He will guide you into all truth; for He will not speak on His own authority, but whatever He hears He will speak; and He will tell you things to come."

In the process of helping me, the Lord did an unexpected work of grace within me. He began to reveal to me...

- Specific types of Christians who will be vulnerable, or susceptible to apostasy.

In the following pages, I have identified those types of Christians, and endeavored to explain why they will be vulnerable.

It is my prayer that all who read the book may be strengthened, and I especially pray that many will be delivered from the paths of apostasy.

Introduction

I grew up in a church that believed in the doctrine of DISPENSATIONALISM.

The word, dispensation, is found only four times in the Bible, all in the New Testament, all in the writings of the Apostle Paul.

The word actually means: *"Management of a household,"* and pertains to stewardship. The Apostle Paul used the word to speak of the responsibility entrusted to him to preach the gospel of Jesus Christ.

Dispensational doctrines vary from church to church, but in the church where I grew up, dispensational teaching was used to neatly divide church history into periods of time.

I remember being taught that God worked in a certain way in past dispensations, but he was now working in a different manner in the present dispensation. Furthermore, we were taught that certain prophetic events would not occur until a future dispensation.

This is how we rejected the experience of being baptized with the Holy Spirit, and the manifestation of speaking in tongues. It was also why we rejected other gifts of the Spirit. We were taught that such experiences were for a different dispensation; specifically, the dispensation of the early church.

Supposedly, when the church entered into the current dispensation, the gifts of the Holy Spirit were no longer needed, and they either passed away, or were withdrawn by God.

Therefore, we felt confident in declaring that modern day manifestations of speaking in tongues, healings, and miracles were not of God, and indeed, were of the devil.

Also, as previously stated, certain events of church history were considered to be part of a future dispensation, which would occur after the so-called rapture of the church.

Specifically, we thought the restoration of Israel would not begin until after the rapture of the church, and would be confined entirely to a seven-year period known as The Great Tribulation.

In addition, many other end time events were also considered to be part of a future dispensation. Events such as: the revealing of the Antichrist, and of course, the subject of this book, THE GREAT APOSTASY.

Consequently, in the church where I grew up, the subject of apostasy was never even mentioned. Our mentality was: *"Soon, the Lord Jesus will rapture us out of the world, and we will miss all the bad stuff."*

I no longer believe in Dispensationalism. It is a man-made doctrine that attempts to compartmentalize God, and limit his power.

Well, I still believe in two dispensations: the dispensation of Old Testament Law prior to the sacrifice of the Lord Jesus Christ, and the dispensation of God's grace because of the sacrifice of Jesus.

Beyond that, the errors of dispensational teaching are quite obvious...

- In recent church history, untold millions of Christians throughout the world have been baptized with the Holy Spirit, and have received the capability to speak with other tongues, as the Holy Spirit gives the utterance.
- Equally so, other gifts of the Spirit are manifested in churches that are open to the moving of the Holy Spirit. I have personally received many healings.

Likewise, teachings that confine certain end time events to a future dispensation are just as glaringly incorrect...

- The Restoration of Israel has obviously begun (re-gathering the people, restoring the land, reviving the people), and the church has not been raptured.
- Whether the Antichrist was alive at the publishing of this book, I do not know. Yet, many centuries past, the Apostle John wrote that the spirit of Antichrist was already at work in the world:

"...every spirit that does not confess that Jesus Christ has come in the flesh is not of God. And this is the spirit of the Antichrist, which you have heard was coming, and is now already in the world." (1 John 4:3).

Similarly, to confine The Great Apostasy to some future period of time is a dangerous choice. Today's world is characterized by an increasing tolerance toward sin, and hostility toward God.

When I was growing up, we heard a lot of preaching about the conviction of the Holy Spirit coming upon people, compelling them to repent of their sins, and accept the Lord. Today, many people have become so hard that the conviction of God's Holy Spirit does not even penetrate their conscience.

Unfortunately, I am not just talking about people in the world. This same tolerance of sin is showing up at church. Among those who call themselves by the name of Jesus Christ, there is a lack of genuine repentance, and increasing hardness toward God.

Perhaps The Great Apostasy will have its fullest expression during the actual time of the Antichrist, but a quick look around you will confirm that apostasy is already at work in many of our churches!

Chapter One

Apostasy Defined

"Now, brethren, concerning the coming of our Lord Jesus Christ and our gathering together to Him, we ask you, not to be soon shaken in mind or troubled, either by spirit or by word or by letter, as if from us, as though the day of Christ had come. Let no one deceive you by any means; for that day will not come unless THE FALLING AWAY COMES FIRST, and the man of sin is revealed, the son of perdition." (2 Thessalonians 2:1-4).

The above scriptures reveal that prior to the return of Jesus Christ, two distinct events will occur...
1) THE FALLING AWAY (the subject of this book), and...
2) THE MAN OF SIN IS REVEALED (also known as the Antichrist).

Interestingly, many Christian books have been written about the End Times...
- ✓ Books about the Antichrist, and the mark of the beast.
- ✓ Books about the restoration of Israel, and the battle of Armageddon.
- ✓ Books that presume to provide us with an exact sequence of end time events.
- ✓ Books warning about God's imminent Judgment,
- ✓ Even books that foolishly predict the day and hour of Christ's return.

Strangely though, not many books have been written about the falling away. Yet, the Bible clearly says, pertaining to the return of Jesus: *"...that day will not come unless the falling away comes first...."*

I believe God has given me insight on why this subject is avoided. End time prophecy can often be taught from a viewpoint of being about those other people – the Antichrist, the false prophets, the enemies of Israel. To the contrary, the falling away is ABOUT US, the church of Jesus Christ!

So, what exactly is the falling away?

By researching reputable New Testament, Greek study helps, we find that the phrase, FALLING AWAY, is *"apostasia,"* or in the English language, APOSTASY.

In fact, the Amplified Bible is so worded from 2 Thessalonians 2:3: *"...that day will not come except the apostasy comes first...."*

By definition, apostasy has the following meanings...
1) A defection from the truth,
2) A revolt against the truth,
3) A falling away from the faith,
4) A departure from the faith.

A similar Greek word, *"apostasion,"* which means *"separation,"* is used in Matthew 19:7 for DIVORCE, as in a marriage relationship; thus, the breaking of a covenant.

Also, the terminology, FALLING AWAY, is not implying that an accident has occurred, such as tripping and falling down. We are talking about rebellion! The NIV states the scripture in this manner: *"...that day will not come until the REBELLION occurs...."*

As previously stated, apostasy has been among us since the inception of the church, although its face has changed through the ages as Satan attempts to deceive each new generation.

However, there is one characteristic that remains the same. Wherever the subject of apostasy appears in the New Testament, the words are not addressed to unbelievers, but rather, to BELIEVERS!

Consider the following…
1) The foundational verses in this chapter begin by saying: *"Now brethren...."*
2) The warning: *"Let no one deceive you by any means..."* about the return of Jesus is obviously for Christians.
3) The same verses also warn the body of Christ about a time of apostasy prior to the return of Jesus.

Such information would be of no concern to unbelievers. They are already away from God, and have neither interest nor belief in the second coming of Jesus Christ.

As we will discover, it is the believer who must be alert to the dangers of apostasy. In fact, apostasy can be further defined as…

A determined, willful rejection of Jesus Christ, and his teachings, by a Christian.

I suppose unbelievers could be indirectly involved in The Great Apostasy. Since the origin of the gospel, the unrighteous have led revolts against the truth.

However, apostasy is primarily a scheme of Satan, aimed directly at believers, trying to cause them to view sin lightly, be offended by the name of Jesus, or anything else that could cause them to depart from the faith.

Think about it; an unbeliever could revolt against the truth, but only a Christian could DEPART FROM THE FAITH.

Let me explain...

- To become a Christian, a person must be SAVED BY FAITH (Ephesians 2:8-9).
- After we become Christians, the Word of God instructs us to LIVE BY FAITH (Hebrews 10:38).
- An unbeliever, who has never entered into the faith, nor lived by faith, could not possibly fall away from the faith!

In the body of Christ, there are Christians who fervently believe in a doctrine of eternal security, sometimes called: ONCE SAVED, ALWAYS SAVED. Such believers would be opposed to the possibility that a Christian could commit apostasy.

Yet, as we continue our exploration of this subject from God's Word, we will clearly see that apostasy includes those who were once numbered among the brethren.

There are also ministers who preach the exact opposite of eternal security, suggesting that one could be repeatedly lost and saved, depending upon their weekly performance.

As we continue our study of apostasy, we will clearly recognize from God's Word, that neither of these positions are correct.

In a later chapter, entitled: *"The Severity of Apostasy,"* we will discover that apostasy has no remedy. It is a condition that cannot be reversed. It is a place of no return!

So, what kind of person could totally turn away from God? In the coming chapters, we will discover some of the answers. For now, let me remind you of what the Lord Jesus said – TO CHRISTIANS – in the church at Laodicea:

"I know your deeds, that you are neither cold nor hot. I wish you were either one or the other! So, because you are lukewarm – neither hot nor cold – I am about to spit you out of my mouth." (Revelation 3:15-16 NIV).

One particular portion of scripture that will help us identify those in danger of apostasy, and a passage we will frequently refer to in this book, is 1 Timothy 4:1-3:

"Now the Spirit EXPRESSLY (clearly, plainly) *says that in latter times some will depart from the faith, giving heed to deceiving spirits and doctrines of demons, speaking lies in hypocrisy, having their own conscience seared with a hot iron, forbidding to marry, and commanding to abstain from foods which God created to be received with thanksgiving by those who believe and know the truth."*

In these verses, four things are identified that could cause someone to depart from the faith...
1) Speaking lies in hypocrisy,
2) Having their conscience seared,
3) Forbidding to marry, and
4) Commanding to abstain from foods.

In time, we will address these issues, but for now, let me identify the ROOT CAUSE of apostasy. The previous verses point out that some will depart from the faith, because of: *"...GIVING HEED* (listening, or paying attention) *to deceiving spirits and doctrines of demons."*

Another translation says: *"...giving heed to SEDUCING SPIRITS..."* (KJV). With both of these descriptions in mind, allow me to amplify the ROOT CAUSE of apostasy...

Christians, who should be listening to God's Word (THE BIBLE)**, will instead listen to seducing, deceiving, evil spirits, and as a result, change their beliefs to doctrines of demons.**

[NOTE: Doctrines of demons can be defined as – Subtle, deceptive teachings, often containing partial truths, which appeal to man's sinful nature, and are intended to seduce believers, and draw them away from pure, unadulterated teaching, which is derived from the whole council of God's Word.]

As we proceed, I will not be judging who has, or has not committed apostasy. Only God knows when a person has crossed that line. He alone is the judge of men's hearts.

My God-appointed responsibilities in the writing of this book are twofold…
1) Identify those Christians – as revealed to me by the Holy Spirit – who will be vulnerable to apostasy.
2) Sound a clear warning in the hope that those who have embarked upon the paths of apostasy will see the error of their way, and repent.

James 5:19-20 is perhaps the passage of scripture that best explains my assignment in the writing of this book:

"Brethren, if anyone among you wanders from the truth, and someone turns him back, let him know that he who turns a sinner from the error of his way will save a soul from death and cover a multitude of sins.

Finally, please understand that The Great Apostasy will happen! God did not direct me to write this book to try and change end time events. He directed me to write the book to WARN HIS PEOPLE!

Chapter Two

Once Saved, Always Saved?

"Therefore consider the goodness and severity of God: on those who fell, severity (Israel's rejection of Jesus), *but toward you, goodness* (Gentiles who accept Jesus), *IF YOU CONTINUE IN HIS GOODNESS. Otherwise you also will be cut off."* (Romans 11:22).

As previously stated, there are segments of the body of Christ who strongly believe in a doctrine of eternal security, also known as: ONCE SAVED, ALWAYS SAVED.

Specifically, this doctrine is the belief that once a person accepts Jesus Christ as their Savior, and experiences forgiveness of sins, they are eternally secure. In other words, it is not possible to either lose, or surrender one's salvation.

Obviously, the doctrine of eternal security is very comforting, but in these increasingly dangerous End Times, as apostasy unfolds before our very eyes, it would be unwise to ignore scriptures that say otherwise.

You see, we have a problem in many of our churches. People are conveniently using the doctrine of eternal security, to convince themselves that they are saved, while at the same time they are purposely living in sin, and have no intention of changing!

Jude, in his short epistle, spoke of people who use the grace of God as a license to sin:

"...certain men whose condemnation was written about long ago have secretly slipped in among you. They are godless men, who CHANGE THE GRACE OF OUR GOD INTO A LICENSE FOR IMMORALITY and deny Jesus Christ our only Sovereign and Lord. Though you already know all this, I want to remind you that the Lord delivered his people out of Egypt, but later destroyed those who did not believe." (Jude 4-5 NIV).

Please notice that the timeless warning in the last sentence of the above verses was delivered to Christians, not non-Christians. In today's church, as in the days of Jude, there are still those who are using the grace of God as a license to sin!

I am not qualified to judge the hearts of such people, as to whether or not they have committed apostasy, but I will boldly declare that those among us who are deliberately living a sinful lifestyle, while hiding behind a doctrine of eternal security, are dangerously close to the path of apostasy.

Perhaps we should take a closer look into this matter of once saved, always saved?

Understanding Covenants

Since the disobedience of Adam and Eve, God has established relationships with man through covenants, including our relationship with God through Jesus Christ. Jesus spoke these words at the last supper:

"For this is My blood of the NEW COVENANT, which is shed for many for the remission of sins." (Matthew 26:28).

A covenant is AN AGREEMENT between two parties, and specifically in our case, an agreement between God and man.

God is not a covenant breaker. Once he establishes a covenant, it is forever, unless he replaces it with a better covenant. For example, God replaced the Old Covenant with the New Covenant (see Hebrews 8:7-13).

From Psalm 89:34, we read of God's faithfulness in keeping covenants:

"My covenant I will not break, nor alter the word that has gone out of My lips."

Yet, even though God is not a covenant breaker, if his covenants with man are to remain in effect, and eternally secure, BOTH PARTIES must maintain the conditions of the covenant.

Isaiah confirmed this fact when he spoke about the children of Israel BREAKING AN EVERLASTING COVENANT:

"The earth is also defiled under its inhabitants, because they have transgressed the laws, changed the ordinance, broken the everlasting covenant." (Isaiah 24:5).

Let me further explain...

Millennia ago, God made a covenant with Abraham, Isaac, and Jacob, to give the land of Israel to their descendants.

Today, we have proof that this covenant is indeed everlasting. God is demonstrating his faithfulness by re-gathering the descendants of Abraham, Isaac, and Jacob from the four corners of the earth, and bringing them back into the land of Israel.

But, listen carefully. Thousands of years passed while the descendants of Abraham, Isaac, and Jacob were scattered throughout the earth because of their unbelief. During that time, literally millions of Jewish people were born, lived their entire lives, and died without ever having set foot in Israel.

Why? Because their forefathers broke the everlasting covenant.

Allow me to be even more direct. Millions of God's chosen people are right now in Hell, not only because their forefathers broke the everlasting covenant that promised them the land, but because they failed to enter into the New Covenant with God through the blood of Jesus Christ.

Jesus himself spoke the following words to his own people:

"For days will come upon you when your enemies will build an embankment around you, surround you and close you in on every side, and level you, and your children within you, to the ground; and they will not leave in you one stone upon another, BECAUSE YOU DID NOT KNOW THE TIME OF YOUR VISITATION." (Luke 19:43-44).

Now, perhaps you are a Gentile believer in Jesus Christ, and you are wondering how, or if such matters pertain to you?

To answer this question, let us look again at our opening scripture in this chapter, and also look at several preceding verses. This passage reveals that God's original chosen people (the Jews) were temporarily cast aside, because of UNBELIEF, and salvation was made available to the Gentiles:

"You will say then, Branches were broken off that I might be grafted in. Well said. Because of unbelief they (Jews) *were broken off, and you* (Gentiles) *stand by faith. Do not be haughty, but fear. For if God did not spare the natural branches, He may not spare you either. Therefore consider the goodness and severity of God: on those who fell, severity; but toward you, goodness, IF YOU CONTINUE IN HIS GOODNESS* (living by grace through faith). *Otherwise you also will be cut off."* (Romans 11:19-22).

Fortunately, in these End Times, we are seeing the beginnings of a spiritual revival among the Jews. One by one, they are being grafted back into the olive tree.

However, what I want you to understand is this – the above scriptures were written to Gentiles, and clearly reveal the possibility of Gentile believers being cut off, if they should stop living by faith in Christ.

Now, maybe you are wondering: *"What about those promises Jesus made to us?"*

"My sheep hear My voice, and I know them, and they follow Me. And I give them eternal life, and they shall never perish; neither shall anyone snatch them out of My hand." (John 10:27-28).

Those promises, and others like them, are God's part (or, his conditions) of the covenant. From God's standpoint, his covenant with us is everlasting, and eternally secure.

However, I repeat, BOTH PARTIES must maintain the conditions of the covenant, or security is forfeited.

~ ~ ~

Let us look even further into this necessity of both parties maintaining the conditions of covenants between God and man.

Romans 1:18-32 is too lengthy to include in this book (please read it for yourself), but this passage of scripture is a clear example of man's failure to keep covenant with God.

Listen to these select verses from the first chapter of Romans, and remember, the Bible is a book for every generation:

"Because, although THEY KNEW GOD (evidently, they were once believers), *they did not glorify Him as God, nor were thankful, but became futile in their thoughts, and their foolish hearts were darkened."* (Romans 1:21).

And, what were the results of their hearts becoming darkened?

"Therefore God also gave them up to uncleanness (sexual impurity, lustful lifestyles), *in the lusts of their hearts, to dishonor their bodies among themselves, who exchanged the truth of God for the lie, and worshiped and served the creature rather than the Creator, who is blessed forever. Amen."* (Romans 1:24-25).

And, besides sexual uncleanness such as fornication and adultery, what else followed the exchanging of truth for lies?

"For this reason God gave them up to VILE PASSIONS (homosexuality – gay and lesbian). *For even their women exchanged the natural use for what is against nature. Likewise also the men, leaving the natural use of the woman, burned in their lust for one another, men with men committing what is shameful, and receiving in themselves the penalty of their error which was due."* (Romans 1:26-27).

And finally, we discover the eventual end of those who become futile in their thoughts; those who exchange the truth of God's Word for lies, and refuse to repent, and fail to keep covenant with God:

"And even as they did not like to retain God in their knowledge, God gave them over to a debased mind (or, reprobate mind), *to do those things which are not fitting."* (Romans 1:28).

That word, DEBASED (reprobate) means: *"Not approved by God; thus rejected."*
Listen to an expanded list of lifestyles that could cause one to become reprobate...

"Being filled with all unrighteousness, fornication, wickedness, covetousness, maliciousness; full of envy, murder, debate, deceit, malignity; whisperers, backbiters, haters of God, despiteful, proud, boasters, inventors of evil things, disobedient to parents, without understanding, COVENANT BREAKERS, without natural affection, implacable, unmerciful." (Romans 1:29-31 KJV).

Did you notice COVENANT BREAKERS are included in the list?

[NOTE: We will further explore covenant breaking in a later chapter entitled: *"The Severity of Apostasy."*]

For now, let us return to our original point in this chapter – Christians deliberately living in sin, refusing to repent, and yet, holding on to a once saved, always saved doctrine.
SUCH CHRISTIANS ARE IN TROUBLE!

Don't jump to conclusions. Just because Christians are living sinful lifestyles does not automatically mean they are apostate. The remedy for sin is repentance, confessing our sins to God, receiving his forgiveness, and allowing him to change our lives.

However, those who persist in living sinful lifestyles are in trouble, because THEY WILL NOT DEAL WITH SIN.

As a result, sin will eventually render them insensitive to conviction from the Holy Spirit, and insensitive to conviction from the Word of God. Their conscience will be in danger of becoming seared.

In time, if they continue in sin, they will come to a place of hardness and unbelief, from which they cannot be brought back to a place of repentance.

Then, listen for the sign of apostasy – that day when they will openly and rebelliously declare...

I no longer believe the Bible; neither do I believe in Jesus Christ. I reject both!

Sadly, the covenant between them and God will be broken!

Chapter Three

Secret Lives

"Now the Spirit expressly (clearly) *says that in latter times some will depart from the faith, giving heed to deceiving* (seducing) *spirits and doctrines of demons, SPEAKING LIES IN HYPOCRISY..."* (1 Timothy 4:1-2).

The biblical definition of HYPOCRISY is: *"Deceit, or acting under a feigned part."* The word also means: *"An answer, or a reply."*

So, hypocrisy is both acting and speaking in an untruthful, deceitful manner; pretending to be someone, or something you are not. Thus, an obvious characteristic of those who depart from the faith is SPEAKING LIES IN HYPOCRISY.

In order to maintain a hypocritical lifestyle, lying would be a necessity, and not just one little fib, but lies upon lies!

Jesus taught us a lot about the hypocrites of his day. Listen to one particular emphasis he made:

"Woe to you, scribes and Pharisees, hypocrites! For you are like whitewashed tombs, which indeed APPEAR BEAUTIFUL OUTWARDLY, but inside are full of dead men's bones and all uncleanness. Even so you also outwardly appear righteous to men, but inside you are full of hypocrisy and lawlessness." (Matthew 23:27-28).

I am sorry to say that there are also many hypocrites in today's churches. People who come to church on Sunday, all dressed up in their Sunday clothes, carrying Bibles in their hands, and singing in the choir. Outwardly, on Sunday, they appear to be godly, but apart from their appearances at church...
- They have a **SECRET LIFE**.

When they go out of town on business, they get drunk on alcohol, gamble away their money, watch pornographic movies on TV, visit sleazy nightclubs and massage parlors, and even hire prostitutes.

Of course, one doesn't have to leave town to watch pornography. They can sit at their computer, in the secrecy of their own home, and dial up pornography on the Internet.

Some who seem to be good, committed, Christian people are engaged in adulterous affairs in secret places.

And, I am not just referring to the regular *"rank and file"* Christians sitting in the church pews. Unfortunately, I am also talking about those in positions of spiritual leadership.

Elders and deacons in the church, who should be providing spiritual guidance, are instead, flirting with, and pursuing vulnerable young women.

Even worse are pastors who prey upon vulnerable young women, and behind closed doors are entangled in numerous adulterous affairs. 2 Timothy 3:6 describes such men:

"They are the kind who worm their way into homes and gain control over weak-willed women, who are loaded down with sins and are swayed by all kinds of evil desires." (NIV).

And, let's not limit our description of those who speak lies in hypocrisy to men only.

There are young ladies, who appear to be part of the vibrancy of the church. Instead, they are motivated by the spirit of Potiphar's wife, and in secret places they are seducing the young men in the church, drawing them away from God, and hindering them from answering the call of God upon their lives.

There are also women in many churches, who are motivated by the spirit of Delilah. Their primary purpose for being in church is to take down the pastor, or seduce others who are in positions of leadership.

Often, such women are actively involved in the church, even serving in positions of ministry. Yet, secretly, the agenda of their heart is not what you see outwardly.

Other women are motivated by the spirit of Jezebel. Outwardly, they may appear to be righteous, but the secret agenda of their heart is to be in control. Often, their desire is to replace the pastor's wife, and become the first lady of the church.

[NOTE: You can read more about these evil spirits that attempt to invade our churches in my book entitled: "GRIEVOUS WOLVES."]

Interestingly, most Christians who have a secret life, also know they will eventually be exposed. Jesus himself taught us:

"...there is nothing covered that will not be revealed, nor hidden that will not be known. Therefore whatever you have spoken in the dark will be heard in the light, and what you have spoken in the ear in inner rooms will be proclaimed on the housetops." (Luke 12:2-3).

All those words spoken – IN THE DARK – IN THE EAR – IN INNER ROOMS – have not escaped the notice of God. In Jeremiah 17:10, God reminds us that he is the judge of men's hearts:

"I, the LORD, search the heart, I test the mind, even to give every man according to his ways, according to the fruit of his doings."

God wants his children to fulfill their full potential in Christ, but this will not happen as long as someone clings to a secret life.

Proverbs 28:13 reminds us of the futility of maintaining a secret life:

"He who covers his sins will not prosper (will not advance, make progress, or succeed), *but whoever confesses and forsakes them will have mercy."*

Some of you may be wondering: *"These Christians who have secret lives, have they already committed apostasy?"*

God is the judge of men's hearts; only he knows when someone has crossed the line. Often times, those who have secret lives just need to repent.

But, HEAR A CLEAR WARNING. Those who persist in maintaining a secret life are definitely in danger of apostasy.

You see, sin never improves a matter; sin always brings further degradation. Someone who refuses to repent will eventually become hardened, and insensitive to sin. No longer will they be sensitive to conviction from the Holy Spirit; no longer will they be sensitive to conviction from God's Word.

And, as we have already discovered, the day could come when they will decide: *"I no longer believe in Jesus Christ! I no longer believe the Bible is God's Word!"*

~ ~ ~

The scriptures tell us that David, King of Israel, was a man after God's own heart:

"…He raised up for them David as king, to whom also He gave testimony and said, I have found David the son of Jesse, a man after My own heart, who will do all My will." (Acts 13:22).

Yet, there was a time when King David had a secret life. He committed adultery with Bathsheba, the wife of Uriah. Later, David had Uriah placed in the forefront of battle, so he would be killed. Then, David could have Bathsheba all for himself (read the entire story in 2 Samuel, chapters 11-12).

Do you remember what happened when Nathan, the prophet confronted David, and uncovered his sin?

David did not attempt to make excuses for his sin, such as…
- *"It was Bathsheba's fault, she seduced me! She purposely exposed herself to entice me. It's her fault!"*

David did not make light of his sin, and act like what he did was insignificant…
- *"Hey, Nathan, let's not put too much importance on this matter. After all, this guy Uriah was a Hittite. He wasn't an Israelite; he wasn't one of us!"*

David did not threaten Nathan, and try to keep his sin secret…
- *"Nathan, you miserable old prophet, if this information goes beyond this room, you are a dead man. You will shortly be visited by Joab, the commander of my army!"*

When David's secret life was exposed, he did not continue speaking lies in hypocrisy; HE REPENTED.

In the 51st Psalm, a psalm of repentance, David said of the Lord:

"Behold, You desire truth in the INWARD PARTS, and in the hidden part You will make me to know wisdom." (Psalm 51:6).

For Christians who are still holding on to secret lives, hear a word from the Lord…

Beware; prophets of the Lord are still roaming the land! The Lord will do his very best to prevent you from committing apostasy, even if he has to openly expose your secret life.

A QUESTION TO PONDER…

Would you prefer to repent now, or be exposed later?

To repent now would bring God's mercy on the scene, and result in forgiveness and cleansing of sin.

Unfortunately, events may have occurred in secret that cannot be reversed. When David's secret life was exposed, Bathsheba was already pregnant. Yet, it is still best to repent now, so God's mercy can bring about restoration to whatever extent possible.

To continue maintaining a secret life, only to be uncovered later, could result in…
1) EMBARRASSMENT,
2) BROKEN RELATIONSHIPS,
3) LOSS OF FAMILY,
4) LOSS OF POSITION, and even
5) LOSS OF MINISTRY.

Worse yet, refusing to repent could place someone another step further along the path to eventual apostasy!

Obviously, now is the time for Christians to surrender their secret lives.

The time has come to be the same person whether you are in church, or out of church.

The time has come to be the same person whether you are in town, or out of town!

It is past time to stop SPEAKING LIES IN HYPOCRISY.

~ ~ ~

One final thought. It is not likely that you will be able to give up a secret life by your own strength. Secret sins, which often seem insignificant in the beginning, have a way of turning into strongholds in people's lives.

Therefore, let us remember the words of the Lord Jesus:

"...you shall receive power when the Holy Spirit has come upon you; and you shall be witnesses to Me..." (Acts 1:8).

Only through the supernatural strength of the Holy Spirit can someone stop speaking lies in hypocrisy, and be delivered from the bondage of a secret life.

Remember, the most effective witness is a person's life, not just his words!

Therefore, my recommendations to those who are living secret lives of sin are twofold:
1) Fall down on your knees before a holy and merciful God, and honestly repent before him, asking his forgiveness and cleansing.
2) Cry out to God to deliver you by the power of his Holy Spirit, and set you free from the bondage of a secret life.

If you have not yet been baptized with the Holy Spirit (as a work of God's grace subsequent to salvation), I highly recommend that you pray for the fullness of God's Holy Spirit.

From 1 Corinthians 14:4, listen to one of the benefits of being baptized with the Holy Spirit:

"He who speaks in a tongue EDIFIES (builds up, strengthens) *himself…"*

The employment of this valuable spiritual gift will help you to obey Proverbs 4:27, and overcome a secret life:

"Do not turn to the right or the left; REMOVE YOUR FOOT FROM EVIL."

Chapter Four

Shipwrecked Faith

"Holding on to (wear like a garment) *faith and a good conscience. Some have rejected these and so have SHIPWRECKED THEIR FAITH. Among them are Hymenaeus and Alexander, whom I have handed over to Satan to be taught not to blaspheme."* (1 Timothy 1:19-20 NIV).

The Apostle Paul writes about two men, Hymenaeus and Alexander, and says they have SHIPWRECKED THEIR FAITH.

Apostasy is the likely result. The idea of suffering shipwreck implies that one did not complete the voyage!

The question is, what exactly caused the faith of these two men to fail?

Besides faith, our opening verses identify another quality – A GOOD CONSCIENCE – and then identify Hymenaeus and Alexander among those whom the Bible says: *"...Some have rejected these...."*

So, in order to understand how faith could become shipwrecked, we need to focus upon A GOOD CONSCIENCE.

[BIBLE DEFINITION: <u>A Good Conscience</u> – Moral consciousness; the capability to distinguish between what is morally good and bad, prompting to do the former and shun the latter.]

[NOTE: As Christians, our standard of morality is the Bible, and especially the teachings of Jesus.]

Perhaps these men once had faith in God, and a good conscience, but the time came when they rejected a good conscience. As a result, their faith suffered shipwreck.

Consequently, Hymenaeus and Alexander can now be included among those described by the Apostle Paul as: *"...having their own CONSCIENCE SEARED with a hot iron."*

The above phrase literally means to mark with a branding iron. A seared conscience is not caused by a momentary incursion into sin due to temptation. We are talking about refusing to repent over a long period of time, and thus, becoming hardened toward sin!

Interestingly, from our opening scriptures, Paul makes one last attempt to rescue these men before giving them up to total apostasy. Listen to his ending remarks: *"...Hymenaeus and Alexander, whom I have handed over to Satan to be taught not to blaspheme."*

Regretfully, the problem was not confined to Paul's day. In today's churches, there are many like Hymenaeus and Alexander, who have also rejected a good conscience!

They fail to distinguish between what is morally good or bad. In some cases, they simply refuse to distinguish between what is morally good or bad. And some, because of a seared conscience, are no longer capable of such discernment.

I regret to report that I am not just talking about young, immature Christians, who are undeveloped in spiritual growth, and could be somewhat excused for temporarily falling. Rather, I am referring to those in leadership within the church, who know God's Word, but have turned away from it.

More and more, we hear of ministers who have dumped their wives of many years, and subsequently married younger women, who are half their age.

Sometimes, these preachers are not even confronted about their sin, and are quickly back in the pulpit, as if nothing happened.

Of course, there are ministers who have not divorced their wives, but in secret places (sometimes in the church office) they are involved in their 7th, 8th, or 9th adulterous affair, often with members of their own church.

These increasingly evil End Times remind us of the days when Hophni and Phinehas, the sons of Eli were serving as priests. From 1 Samuel 2:22, we read the following:

"Now Eli was very old; and he heard everything his sons did to all Israel, and how they lay with the women who assembled at the door of the tabernacle of meeting."

Of even more concern are those ministers who are giving heed to seducing spirits, and succumbing to homosexual encounters, and entering into homosexual relationships.

And, just when you think things could not possibly get any worse, we hear of Catholic priests who are preying upon, and sexually molesting young boys.

I am reminded of the words of the Lord Jesus in Matthew 18:6:

"...whoever causes one of these little ones who believe in Me to sin, it would be better for him if a millstone were hung around his neck, and he were drowned in the depth of the sea."

Did you hear what Jesus said? He said it would be BETTER; it would actually be an IMPROVEMENT in someone's life to have a millstone hung around their neck, and be drowned in the depth of the sea, than to cause a little one (a child, or new Christian) who believes in Jesus to commit sin!

Why? Because all too often, it causes the little one to also depart from the faith!

Strangely, ministers sometimes work hard to justify sin in their lives, even misusing the scriptures in an effort to do so.

I once heard of a ridiculous explanation from a certain preacher who was attempting to justify sin in his life...
- Because King David had concubines, it was also acceptable for him to have multiple sexual affairs.

Equally ridiculous was the missionary who was dismissed from his post for having sex with young girls. His explanation...
- If one has sex with girls under the age of 18, it's not ADULTery.

Then, we have ministers who employ the God-sanctioned explanation...
- *"When I married my first wife, I made a terrible mistake. I was out of the will of God."*

Of course, now that they have dumped the old wife, and married the young girl, they are finally in the will of God. At last, they are married to the woman ordained by God!

I would be afraid to stand before God and man, and tell such lies! Do ministers have no fear of God?

From the Apostle Paul's sermon on Mars Hill, the following words of advice would fit in very appropriately here:

"In the past (before people were indwelt by the Holy Spirit) *God overlooked such ignorance, but now he commands all people everywhere to repent."* (Acts 17:30 NIV).

Then again, some ministers don't bother with trying to justify sin; they just ignore the Word of God altogether. They view themselves as indispensable, and have the same attitude as the church at Corinth when Paul confronted them about sin: *"...you are proud and arrogant! And you ought rather to mourn..."* (from 1 Corinthians 5:2 AMP).

To be sure, many of God's people depart from such churches, or stop supporting such ministries. They refuse to sit under a pastor who is unrepentant, or support a ministry that ignores sin. What puzzles me is the people who stay?

Soon, they are once again shouting and dancing in the church, and giving the Lord's tithe, and their offerings into a house of sin.

~ ~ ~

You may wonder how someone, who is called by God, could deteriorate to such an immoral state that their conscience becomes seared as with a hot iron?

Of course, the lust of the flesh obviously plays a big role. James 1:14 tells us:

"But every man is tempted, when he is drawn away of his own lust, and enticed." (KJV).

Even a member of Paul's missionary team was lured away by the lust of the flesh:

"...Demas has forsaken me, having loved this present world, and has departed for Thessalonica..." (2 Timothy 4:10).

Yet, I am convinced that in today's church there is even a bigger trap than the lust of the flesh. I am speaking of pride and ego.

In this age of instant visibility, due to TV, books, or the Internet, ministers can become so popular, so powerful, so wealthy, and so much in demand, that they see themselves as indispensable to the kingdom of God, and no longer subject to the laws of God.

Now, maybe some of you are questioning: *"Some of the ministers who sinned said they have repented. Should we not forgive them, and allow them to resume their ministry?"*

I certainly recognize that there is a place in the body of Christ for genuine repentance, and also definitely a place for someone to be restored to a position of ministry.

But, let's continue to be honest. I am very suspicious of ministers who explain how they got away from God, and in their backslidden condition they just happened to dump the old wife, and marry the young girl. Then, they make this great announcement: *"I repented, and came back to God!"*

Just declaring: *"I have repented,"* could be a convenient way to smooth things over, and patch things up, after someone has made a planned, deliberate excursion into sin to get what their flesh wanted.

Actions, not words, should prove whether or not a person has repented. Matthew 3:8, from the Amplified Bible says:

> *"Bring forth fruit* (actions, not just words) *that is consistent with repentance – let your lives prove your change of heart."*

[NOTE: More about this later in the chapter entitled: *"The Way of Repentance."*]

Teaching Heresy

Interestingly, Hymenaeus, one of the men whose faith suffered shipwreck, is apparently mentioned again in 2 Timothy 2:16-18:

"But shun profane and idle babblings, for they will increase to more ungodliness. And their message will spread like cancer. Hymenaeus and Philetus are of this sort, who have strayed concerning the truth, saying that the resurrection is already past; and they OVERTHROW THE FAITH OF SOME."

Did you notice what they were teaching? They were saying: *"...the resurrection is already past..."* obviously referring to the resurrection of the dead when Jesus returns.

This is the same warning the Apostle Paul gave to the church in 2 Thessalonians 2:1-3, our foundational scriptures for this book:

"Now, brethren, concerning the coming of our Lord Jesus Christ and our gathering together to Him, we ask you, not to be soon shaken in mind or troubled, either by spirit or by word or by letter, as if from us, as though the day of Christ had come. Let no one deceive you by any means; for that Day will not come unless the falling away (the apostasy) *comes first...."*

And, so it is with those who have rejected a good conscience. Soon thereafter, they will be teaching heresy.

I heard about a man who was delivered from homosexuality, and began to travel as an evangelist. For a number of years, he had an effective ministry. But then, things began to change.

First, he started traveling with young men, which because of his background was not advisable. Then, he began to teach that in the end, everyone would be saved.

Perhaps he had once again succumbed to homosexuality, and was trying to justify sin in his life. Regardless, the man was teaching heresy.

In the case of Hymenaeus and Philetus, the results of their heretical teachings were devastating. 2 Timothy 2:18 says: *"...they overthrow the faith of some."*

Another translation says: *"...they destroy the faith of some"* (NIV).

Not only was their own faith shipwrecked, but now, they are causing the faith of others to become shipwrecked as well. Herein is the greatest tragedy when church leaders reject a good conscience...

The shipwrecked faith of those who were following their spiritual guidance.

Regretfully, after a minister has blatantly entered into moral failure, and refuses to repent, many of the sheep in their fold do not find other churches. They just drop out of church altogether.

Ministers in today's church should learn a lesson from the Old Testament qualifications for the priesthood:

"And they shall teach My people the difference between the holy and the unholy, and cause them to discern between the unclean and the clean." (Ezekiel 44:23).

A GOOD CONSCIENCE IS NOT LIMITED TO SEXUAL SINS

The rejection of a good conscience is not limited to sexual sins. A leader could reject a good conscience in the acquiring, or handing of money. Listen to these familiar scriptures:

"But those who desire to be rich fall into temptation and a snare, and into many foolish and harmful lusts which drown men in destruction and perdition. For the love of money is a root of all kinds of evil, for which SOME HAVE STRAYED FROM THE FAITH in their greediness, and pierced themselves through with many sorrows." (1 Timothy 6:8-10).

A good friend, who is also in the ministry, shared about attending a large church with more than 10,000 members. Three offerings were taken; one for the church, and two for the pastor.

During the offerings for the pastor, the people were instructed not to write checks, but to give cash only. Was the pastor trying to avoid personal income taxes?

The offerings for the pastor were not quiet affairs. The offering buckets were not simply passed down the aisles. Much fanfare was employed as people were streaming forward to the front of the church, and announcing how much they were giving.

By simple arithmetic, my friend estimated that at least $1,000,000.00 (that's one million dollars) was handed directly to the pastor that night. And, my friend was told that this was a regular occurrence in the church!

I don't know what the pastor did with the money. God is the judge. However, it would seem to me that if a minister stuffed millions of dollars into his own pockets, while ignoring other needs in the body of Christ, he could likely be numbered among those who have rejected a good conscience!

Again, I am not qualified to judge whether or not someone has committed apostasy, but I am responsible to sound the warning.

Now, hear a word from the Lord…

The days are coming when you will see apostasy with your own eyes, and hear it with your own ears. Well-known, highly visible ministers, whom you thought were pillars of the faith, will stand and declare that they no longer believe the Bible; they no longer believe in Jesus Christ.

Jesus once said, about these End times:

"So be on your guard; I have told you everything ahead of time." (Mark 13:23 NIV).

God provides us with a fearful description of those who were entrusted with leadership, but later rejected a good conscience:

"If they have escaped the corruption of the world by knowing our Lord and Savior Jesus Christ, and are again entangled in it, and overcome, they are worse off at the end than they were at the beginning. It would have been better for them not to have known the way of righteousness, than to have known it and then to turn their backs on the sacred command that was passed on to them. Of them the proverbs are true: A dog returns to its vomit, and, a sow that is washed goes back to her wallowing in the mud." (2 Peter 2:20-22 NIV).

In conclusion, let's recall, and emphasize something from our opening verses in this chapter. We are instructed to HOLD ON to two things…
- FAITH, and
- A GOOD CONSCIENCE.

Most Christians know how to hold on to faith. If they have a financial need, or if they need healing, they will search the scriptures, find a promise that meets their need, call for the elders of the church, get anointed with oil, and ask everyone in sight to agree with them in prayer.

Then, they will hold on to the promises of God's Word, and hold on to the prayers that were spoken over them, like a vise grip until God meets their need.

This is good. Christians should hold on to faith. In fact, the Bible tells us that without faith, it is impossible to please God!

Yet, in these increasingly evil End Times, as apostasy has begun to rage through our churches, it is equally important to…

HOLD ON TO A GOOD CONSCIENCE!

Chapter Five

Forbidding to Marry

"Now the Spirit expressly (clearly) *says that in latter times some will depart from the faith, giving heed to deceiving spirits and doctrines of demons … FORBIDDING TO MARRY…"* (1 Timothy 4:1-3).

The word, FORBIDDING, in our opening scriptures means: *"To hinder, or to prevent,"* as well as to forbid.

Therefore, FORBIDDING TO MARRY can also be accurately stated as…

- Hindering marriage from being exactly what God intended, when he originally established the marriage relationship during creation.
- Working against marriage, preventing it from being godly, or successful.

Marriage was God's idea; in the beginning he established the marriage relationship, and set in order, the law of nature. Listen to the following scriptures as God literally created marriage:

"And the LORD God said, It is not good that man should be alone; I will make him a helper comparable to him ... And the LORD God caused a deep sleep to fall on Adam, and he slept; and He took one of his ribs, and closed up the flesh in its place. Then the rib which the LORD God had taken from man He made into a woman, and He brought her to the man. And Adam said: This is now bone of my bones and flesh of my flesh; she shall be called Woman, because she was taken out of Man. Therefore a man shall leave his father and mother and be joined to his wife, and they shall become one flesh." (Genesis 2:18, 21-24).

Ever since that time, Satan has tried to destroy, or distort the marriage relationship in an effort to hinder God's plan, and prevent marriage from being successful.

Satan hates marriage. In the physical, or natural realm, it is the closest relationship we have that compares to our relationship in the Spirit with Jesus Christ. Like our relationship with the Lord, marriage is also based on a covenant. Listen to Ephesians 5:31-32:

"For this reason a man shall leave his father and mother and be joined to his wife, and the two shall become one flesh. This is a great mystery, but I speak concerning Christ and the church."

In his attempts to destroy, or distort the covenant of marriage, Satan's schemes are many, and varied...

- Certain church organizations, in direct violation of the Word of God, put forth a pretense of holiness by forbidding their ministers to marry.
- Among those who marry, the divorce rate is soaring. Marriage covenants are dissolved on a whim, often citing obscure reasons, like incompatibility, to justify divorce. Selfishness reigns!
- Thousands of unmarried couples mock God by living together, and engaging in sexual relations outside the bonds of matrimony.
- Hardcore feminists degrade marriage, and in particular, degrade God's order in marriage, because it requires wives to submit to their husbands.
- Homosexuals – both those misnamed as *"Gays,"* and lesbians – are distorting the marriage covenant by entering into same-sex marriages, which God will never sanction.

An Even Worse Problem

So, how does this pertain to apostasy?

Destroying the marriage covenant is bad enough, but there is something even worse than broken relationships, failed marriages, sexual perversion, and scattered children.

I am talking about the eternal destination of one's spirit and soul; specifically speaking of those who reject Jesus Christ, and are cut off from God's presence.

Such is the end result of apostasy, and as we shall see, some will actually depart from the faith, and commit apostasy, because…

- They are forbidden to marry,
- Their marriage is perverted, hindered, or prevented from being successful.
- They just treat the ordinance of God as worthless, or unimportant.

Take a look around you…

Do ministers who are forbidden to marry by their church always valiantly abstain from sexual entanglements?

When marriages are torn apart by divorce, do both parties continue to serve God with all their hearts?

Do couples living together, and sexually involved outside of wedlock go to the mission field?

The fact is, any destruction, distortion, or forbidding of the marriage relationship is also potentially a departure from the faith.

As an example, let us focus upon divorce. In Malachi 2:16, the Bible says GOD HATES DIVORCE. Listen to one reason why:

"...the LORD has been witness between you and the wife of your youth, with whom you have dealt treacherously; yet she is your companion and your wife by covenant. But did He not make them one, having a remnant of the Spirit? And why one? HE SEEKS GODLY OFFSPRING..." (Malachi 2:14-15).

God knows that divorce is likely to scatter the children, and worse yet, potentially cause them to depart from the faith. And, after they have turned away from God, apostasy lies at the door!

Think about it; do the children of broken homes always draw closer to God?

~ ~ ~

As a second example, let us focus upon Catholic priests, who have been found guilty of molesting young boys (although the problem is not limited to the Catholic Church).

Obviously, some of those priests were evil men, who should never have been allowed to enter the priesthood.

Yet, I am sure the Catholic Church could have avoided some of these problems if their priests were allowed to marry.

God has a solution for sexual immorality. It's called marriage:

"...because of sexual immorality, let each man have his own wife, and let each woman have her own husband." (1 Corinthians 7:2).

And, what of those young boys who were molested? Since growing into adults, how many of them are preaching the gospel?

One such individual, during a television interview, said of the priest who molested him: *"He destroyed my faith!"*

~ ~ ~

As previously explained in chapter two, our relationship with God is based upon a covenant. Likewise, the marriage relationship is also based upon a covenant.

When one breaks covenant with God, and denies the Lord Jesus Christ, it results in apostasy.

When Christians destroy, or distort their marriage covenant, it may not immediately result in apostasy. However, it definitely has the potential of causing one, or both parties to depart from the faith, and embark upon the road to apostasy.

Do not be deceived by worldly counselors who ignore God's original plan for marriage, and advise us to dissolve marriages, distort them, or not bother with marriage at all.

Broken covenants, distorted relationships, and refusing to obey the laws of God do not improve one's life. Eventually, such actions will result in devastation.

I realize that God allows for divorce in the case of sexual infidelity, but Christians must be extremely careful about hastily divorcing their spouse, and hastily entering into other marriage relationships. Jesus taught us:

"...whoever divorces his wife (or, whoever divorces her husband), *EXCEPT FOR SEXUAL IMMORALITY, and marries another, commits adultery; and whoever marries her who is divorced commits adultery"* (Matthew 19:9).

In these increasingly evil End Times, the devil will be using every conceivable scheme to cause Christians to become offended at God, and depart from the faith.

One evil tactic Satan will repeatedly use is attempting to destroy the marriage covenant, or twisting it in every distorted, perverted way imaginable.

Unfortunately, some will fall away from the faith because of these wicked schemes.

In conclusion to this chapter, as in former chapters, I am not able to judge who has, or has not committed apostasy. My assignment remains the same – sound the warning!

For those contemplating...
- Forbidding the marriage relationship,
- Hindering, or preventing the success of marriage,
- Distorting the marriage relationship, or
- Severing the marriage covenant without scriptural grounds,

I would challenge you to think twice. It could ultimately determine your eternal destination, as well as the eternal destination of those whom you wound!

God's way is better. His instructions on marriage, throughout the Bible, never lead toward the paths of apostasy!

Chapter Six

Abstaining from Foods

"Now the Spirit expressly (clearly) *says that in latter times some will depart from the faith, giving heed to deceiving spirits and doctrines of demons ... COMMANDING TO ABSTAIN FROM FOODS which God created to be received with thanksgiving by those who believe and know the truth. For every creature of God is good, and nothing is to be refused if it is received with thanksgiving; for it is sanctified by the word of God and prayer."* (1 Timothy 4:1-5).

How strange! The Bible actually says that commanding people to abstain from foods could be a factor in causing them to depart from the faith; thereby putting them in danger of apostasy.

How could what we eat, or abstain from eating, possibly play a role in whether or not our relationship with God remains intact?

In the Old Testament, God's people were required to follow certain food laws. Under the New Covenant, Christians (both Jews and Gentiles) are not required to obey those laws:

"For the kingdom of God is not eating and drinking, but righteousness and peace and joy in the Holy Spirit." (Romans 14:17).

Perhaps the Apostle Paul was addressing this matter in our opening scriptures? Yet, because the Bible is a book that applies to every generation, there must be something more the Holy Spirit is trying to tell us.

~ ~ ~

I once had the opportunity to sit under the teaching of a pastor from India. He taught a revealing lesson on how Hinduism has been cleverly imported to America under the guise of the New Age Movement.

Subsequently, he explained, the New Age Movement has crept into the church under the guise of personal health.

In particular, this pastor emphasized that vegetarianism in India has absolutely nothing to do with good health. To the contrary, it is a doctrine of the Hindu religion!

Specifically, Hindu doctrine teaches that all life is sacred, based upon their belief in reincarnation. A Hindu does not eat meat, because a cow might be his reincarnated grandmother.

This pastor further explained that in India there are more dedicated Hindus, known as Vegans. These folks do not eat meat, and they also do not eat animal by-products (such as milk, eggs, cheese, ice cream, etc.).

He also explained that there are Hindus even more dedicated than Vegans. These poor souls will not cook food, lest they kill bacteria. They go around begging for food, with the belief that if someone else cooks the food, and kills the bacteria, the sin will be upon the head of that other person.

The underlying message of vegetarianism is the Hindu philosophy that all life is sacred; thus, the false concept of multiple gods. To the contrary, God clearly states:

"...Before Me there was no God formed, nor shall there be after Me. I, even I, am the LORD, and besides Me there is no Savior." (Isaiah 43:10-11).

So, how are these matters a problem to Christians? After all, health food advocates in the body of Christ are not teaching us to believe in many gods!

In the body of Christ, we are increasingly hearing teachings which insist that we must eat in a certain manner, or WE ARE NOT PLEASING GOD.

These teachings sound really important, and often emphasize the fact that our bodies are the temple of the Holy Spirit. Therefore, we must eat in a certain manner in order to take proper care of God's dwelling place.

1 Corinthians 3:16-17 is one passage of scripture that is incorrectly used to back up these teachings:

"Do you not know that you are the temple of God and that the Spirit of God dwells in you? If anyone DEFILES THE TEMPLE of God, God will destroy him. For the temple of God is holy, which temple you are."

Just listening to some of these Christian health food Gurus, one could almost get the idea that salvation is through nutrition.

The deeper one gets into these teachings, the more convinced they could become that eating a specified diet is the most important issue of the Christian life.

New Christians, and immature Christians, who are vulnerable to every wind of doctrine, could easily begin to think like Hindus – that all life is sacred, and the eating of animals is disgusting!

The teachings of Jesus completely refute such doctrines. In Matthew 15:11, he said:

"Not what goes into the mouth defiles a man; but what comes out of the mouth, this defiles a man."

Later, he further explained these matters to his disciples:

"Do you not yet understand that whatever enters the mouth goes into the stomach and is eliminated? But those things which proceed out of the mouth come from the heart, AND THEY DEFILE A MAN. For out of the heart proceed evil thoughts, murders, adulteries, fornications, thefts, false witness, blasphemies." (Matthew 15:17-19).

GETTING THE FACTS STRAIGHT

1) GOD DID NOT COMMAND US TO EAT ONLY FRUITS AND VEGETABLES.

Those who teach us to abstain from foods like to quote Genesis 1:29:

"Then God said, I give you every seed-bearing plant on the face of the whole earth and every tree that has fruit with seed in it. They will be yours for food." (NIV).

They forget to tell us about Genesis 9:2-3:

"The fear and dread of you will fall upon all the beasts of the earth and all the birds of the air, upon every creature that moves along the ground, and upon all the fish of the sea; they are given into your hands. Everything that lives and moves will be food for you. Just as I gave you the green plants, I now give you everything." (NIV).

Some explain that the above verses were immediately after Noah and his family exited the ark, and since all vegetation had been destroyed by the flood, God temporarily gave them permission to eat meat.

Yet, there is no indication in the scriptures that God gave Noah permission to eat meat only until he and his children could plant and harvest gardens.

In time, God instituted certain Feasts of the Lord. In the Passover, the eating of meat was required.

2) JESUS WAS NOT A VEGETARIAN.

I have heard people argue that Jesus was a vegetarian. Yet, from the Bible we clearly know that Jesus ate lamb, because he ate the Passover with his disciples. Listen to the scriptures from Mark 14:12:

"Now on the first day of Unleavened Bread, when they killed the Passover lamb, His disciples said to Him, Where do You want us to go and prepare, that You may eat the Passover?"

We also know from the Bible that Jesus ate fish, even after he was resurrected from the dead. He once said to his disciples:

"...Have you any food here? So they gave Him a piece of a broiled fish and some honeycomb. And He took it and ate in their presence." (from Luke 24:41-43).

3) HINDERING THE GREAT COMMISSION.

Insisting on following a specified diet, and refusing to eat certain foods, could actually cause someone to disobey God, and fail to answer his calling upon their life.

Listen, as Jesus gave commandments to his disciples when he sent them to preach the Gospel:

"Whatever city you enter, and they receive you, eat such things as are set before you." (Luke 10:8).

I can almost hear Christians complaining about the above scripture: *"But, what if I eat something that makes me sick?"*

We must learn to live by faith in God's Word. Listen again, as Jesus sent forth his disciples to preach the Gospel, this time into all the world:

"And these signs will follow those who believe: In My name they will cast out demons; they will speak with new tongues; they will take up serpents (exercise authority over Satan and demons); *and IF THEY DRINK ANYTHING DEADLY, it will by no means hurt them; they will lay hands on the sick, and they will recover."* (Mark 16:17-18).

Set Free by the Truth

Under the New Covenant, Christians have the freedom to eat as they choose, without displeasing God. Listen to these instructions from God's Word:

"One man's faith allows him to eat everything, but another man, whose faith is weak, eats only vegetables. The man who eats everything must not look down on him who does not, and the man who does not eat everything must not condemn the man who does, for God has accepted him ... He who eats meat, eats to the Lord, for he gives thanks to God; and he who abstains, does so to the Lord and gives thanks to God." (Romans 14:2-3, 6 NIV).

So, be free to choose whatever foods you prefer, but remember two things…
1) Never make a doctrine out of your diet,
2) Do not offend your brother or sister in Christ over something as insignificant as food (Please read the entire 14th chapter of Romans).

LEARNING TO LIVE BY FAITH

"For everything God created is good, and nothing is to be rejected if it is received with thanksgiving, because it is CONSECRATED (sanctified) *by the word of God and prayer."* (1 Timothy 4:4-5 NIV).

If we are willing to live by faith, specifically by believing and practicing the above verses of scripture, the food we eat can actually be sanctified (set apart for our nutrition, thus purified) by the authority of God's Word, and through our prayers of thanksgiving.

Besides the above verses, here is another promise from God's Word that you can claim for the sanctification of your food:

"So you shall serve the LORD your God, and He will bless your bread and your water. And I will take sickness away from the midst of you." (Exodus 23:25).

Now, I do admit that some of our so-called foods would be hard pressed to qualify as: *"...EVERYTHING GOD CREATED...."* Some of the foods on our supermarket shelves have been processed beyond recognition. Others foods fall into the category of junk foods, and are proven to be unhealthy.

Personally, I like to eat a diet consisting of natural foods, rather than processed foods, but I don't preach this preference as if it were a part of the Gospel of Jesus Christ.

Sometimes, I travel to foreign countries in order to fulfill the ministry to which God has called me. The foods I prefer are not always available in these countries, and I must eat what is set before me.

I live by faith during these times. Through my belief in God's Word, and by my prayers of thanksgiving, I always trust in the Lord to sanctify whatever I eat.

So, be free to eat the healthiest foods you can find, but regardless, choose to live by faith. Do not waste your days worrying about food. Listen to these instructions:

"Do not be carried about with various and strange doctrines. For it is good that the heart be established by grace, not with foods which have not profited those who have been occupied with them." (Hebrews 13:9).

Be Thankful

Most important, always be thankful to God for his provision. Do not be like the children of Israel, who complained, even though God provided them with Manna every morning.

I have observed those who are occupied with foods, and fearful about their diet. Quite often, they are not thankful people.

Sometimes, they are angry people. Angry about the way food is grown, angry about the ingredients in food, angry about the way food is processed, and highly offended that everyone else does not agree with them.

I even know of Christians who were visibly upset at the church potluck, and voiced their disapproval, because foods were served that they considered to be unhealthy.

Christians with unthankful attitudes should repent of their selfishness, and be reminded that most people in the world do not have the luxury of shopping at health food stores, or eating specially grown organic foods.

In fact, many of our brethren in the Lord literally trust God to: *"Give us this day our daily bread."* (Matthew 6:11).

Rather than being selfish, unthankful, and daily occupied with foods, they should seek out ways to help the poor, and feed those who are hungry!

Strangely, in these deceptive End Times, many will give heed to deceiving spirits and doctrines of demons, and get all stressed out over foods. They will enter into bondage for themselves, and try to put others in bondage by commanding them to abstain from foods.

Many will follow these totally unnecessary teachings, and some who once thought the redemptive work of the Lord Jesus was the most important issue of the Christian life, will begin to think diet is the most important.

Some will become so offended over food, because everyone does not agree with their values, that they will become angry at other Christians, angry at the church, and even angry at God. People will actually turn back, and stop following God, over something as insignificant as food!

In conclusion, let's once again emphasize what God emphasizes:

"For the kingdom of God is not eating and drinking, but righteousness and peace and joy in the Holy Spirit. For he who serves Christ in these things (righteousness, peace, joy) *IS ACCEPTABLE TO GOD and approved by men."* (Romans 14:17-18).

Chapter Seven

Comfort Zones

"For the time will come when they will not endure sound doctrine, but according to their own desires, because they have itching ears, they will heap up for themselves teachers; and they will turn their ears away from the truth, and be turned aside to fables." (2 Timothy 4:3-4).

According to the above verses, a time will come when people (church people, who listen to preaching and teaching) will not endure sound doctrine, because they have ITCHING EARS (ears that want to be tickled). They will reject teaching that is unpleasant to the hearing.

As a result, *"...they will turn their ears away from the truth, and be turned aside to FABLES"* (myths, and man-made fictions). They will choose to live in a SPIRITUAL FANTASYLAND.

I have had the privilege of visiting quite a few churches, and I am pleased to report that there are many good churches.

However, there are also churches where the people have succumbed to itching ears. The pastor, and others in leadership preach only what is pleasant, or comfortable to the hearing of the people.

Even guest speakers are carefully chosen to echo only what the pastor is preaching: *"...according to their own desires ... they will heap up for themselves teachers...."*

Without realizing it, the leadership in such churches could be endangering their flock, and actually causing them to be susceptible to apostasy. The Apostle Paul once wrote:

"For I have not shunned (avoided, concealed due to cowardice) *to declare to you the whole counsel of God."* (Acts 20:27).

From 2 Timothy 3:16, Paul also taught: *"ALL SCRIPTURE ... IS PROFITABLE for doctrine* (or, teaching), *for reproof* (or, conviction), *for correction, for instruction in righteousness."*

Church leaders who avoid uncomfortable portions of the Bible are training their people to develop itching ears. Equally so, none of God's Word should be concealed, or hidden from the people due to cowardice!

We could go in many directions here, in order to explore the dangers of itching ears. I have selected a page from my own spiritual development.

There was a time when I only wanted to hear teachings on SUCCESS, BLESSINGS, and PROSPERITY.

The books I read, the teaching tapes to which I listened, the seminars I attended, the Bible promises I memorized, were mostly on success, blessings, and prosperity.

If someone preached a message about enduring hardship as a good soldier in God's army, I immediately tuned them out. I did not want the Christian life to be difficult; I wanted it to be comfortable!

From 2 Timothy 4:5, Paul once wrote to his spiritual son, Timothy:

"But you be watchful in all things, ENDURE AFFLICTIONS (suffer hardship, endure troubles), *do the work of an evangelist, fulfill your ministry."*

Now, listen carefully…

As we progress further into these End Times, there will be a greater need to develop our faith in God's Word to endure hardship, than developing our faith to be more comfortable.

Although the following words spoken by Jesus are not limited to the End Times, they definitely apply to them:

"If the world hates you, keep in mind that it hated me first. If you belonged to the world, it would love you as its own. As it is, you do not belong to the world, but I have chosen you out of the world. That is why the world hates you." (John 15:18-19 NIV).

Prior to his second coming, it will become more and more unpopular to be a follower of Jesus Christ. Those who are following Jesus just to claim the Bible promises for success, blessings, and prosperity will not be happy about persecution.

Please, don't misunderstand me. Without doubt, I believe in all the promises of God's Word, including the promises for success, blessings, and prosperity.

The Lord has called me into the ministry. I certainly want my ministry to be a success, not a failure!

I actively seek out the promises of God's Word, and claim them by faith, in order to experience the blessings of God.

Without financial prosperity from the hand of God, I could not accomplish what the Lord has called me to do.

Yet, if all I want to hear from God's Word is success, blessings, and prosperity, I have itching ears. Likely, my motives will become selfish, and my judgments will reflect what is most comfortable for me.

Once while attending a seminar that was heavy on success, blessings, and prosperity, a lady rushed up to me during one of the brief breaks, and excitedly declared: *"We are going to have two Cadillac's, one for me, and one for my husband!"*

I responded with a faint, *"Praise the Lord,"* and she went on to explain: *"The Bible says we can have what we say, and I say that we are going to have two Cadillac's."*

I later wondered why she did not rush up to me, with equal enthusiasm, and proclaim: *"The Bible says we can have what we say, and I say that we are going to double our giving to World Missions this year!"*

~ ~ ~

So, how does this apply to apostasy? As I previously shared, the Lord has revealed to me, certain types of Christians who will be vulnerable to apostasy. One such type is…

Those who develop their faith in God's Word only for the purpose of being more comfortable, and fail to develop their faith to endure hardship!

By hardship, I am not talking about being sick, financially broke, and beat up by Satan, although you may have to engage in spiritual warfare over those matters.

Rather, I am talking about going against the compromising standards of this world, and suffering persecution and tribulation for the name of the Lord Jesus Christ. Being more specific…

- Standing up for righteousness, refusing to be tolerant of false religions, and continuing to declare that Jesus Christ is the only way to God.
- Holding fast to the unchanging Word of God, refusing to compromise the truth, upholding the integrity of the Bible.
- Refusing to be tolerant of sin, or view sin lightly. Continuing to distinguish between good and evil.

Sadly, some who are following Jesus just for the blessings will not be willing to stand in the evil day. They will turn back when things become uncomfortable!

Now, don't forget, I believe the promises of God's Word, including those for success, blessings, and prosperity. Yet, as we have already discovered, too much emphasis on money, and the comforts of this life, can lead toward apostasy (see 1 Timothy 6:9-10).

Let's explore another direction in which Christians are likely to lose their comfort.

We are living during exciting times, when the Lord has begun the Restoration of Israel. Specifically…
- God is re-gathering his original chosen people, the descendants of Abraham, Isaac, and Jacob.
- He is bringing them back to the land of Israel, which he promised by covenant to their fathers.
- For the ultimate purpose of spiritually reviving them (read Ezekiel 36:24-28).

At the same time, Satan is stirring up fundamentalist Muslims to attack Israel in a frantic, but unsuccessful effort to prevent the scriptures from being fulfilled.

Increasingly, these attacks will be directed not just at Israel, but against all who stand with Israel, including Christians.

Jesus said to his original disciples, and to us, pertaining to tribulation and persecution:

"All this I have told you SO THAT YOU WILL NOT GO ASTRAY. They will put you out of the synagogue; in fact, a time is coming when anyone who kills you will think he is offering a service to God. They will do such things because they have not known the Father or me." (John 16:1-3 NIV).

Being put out of the synagogue obviously applied to Jews who accepted Jesus Christ (and still applies), but listen again to a portion of the above scriptures:

"...A time is coming when anyone who kills you will think he is offering a service to God."

Strangely, these fundamentalist Muslims, who are attacking Israel, and also attacking Christians, believe they are serving God by doing so. What great deception!

As things become more and more difficult, some who currently call themselves by the name of Christ will not be willing to stand with Israel, because it may potentially place them in harm's way, or may require them to endure hardship.

As pressure increases against Israel, and threats multiply against those who stand with God's Word on this issue, watch for so-called Christians to turn their backs against Israel, and even deny Bible prophecies that promise God's restoration of his chosen people.

And, this they will do, simply because they are uncomfortable, and unwilling to endure hardship for the sake of God's kingdom!

Sadly, this will put them into a position of FIGHTING AGAINST GOD, and it could lead them into the paths of apostasy.

Developing our Faith

Perhaps you are wondering: *"Exactly how does someone develop their faith in God's Word to endure hardship, and survive these tumultuous End Times?"*

May I recommend that you read, study, and memorize the 91st Psalm. Then, obey the instruction in verse 2:

"I will SAY of the Lord, He is my refuge and my fortress; my God, in Him I will trust."

Notice that the above scripture instructs us to SAY OF THE LORD! We must boldly confess God's promises in the 91st Psalm; especially the promises that provide for our safety, protection, and deliverance.

By doing so, you will prepare yourself to be counted among those described by the Lord Jesus in Luke 21:36:

"Watch therefore, and pray always that you may be counted worthy to escape all these things that will come to pass, and to stand before the Son of Man."

Did you notice the expression, COUNTED WORTHY? It means: *"To prevail against, or overpower."* God intends for us to overcome hardship, not be overcome by it!

These are not the days for trying to live in a spiritual fantasyland, and pretending that ALL IS WELL.

These are the days for developing one's faith to endure hardship for the sake of the kingdom of God.

The End Times will be a time of great victory for the kingdom of God. Ancient Bible prophecies will continue to be fulfilled, and completed, in preparation for the return of the Lord Jesus Christ.

For those who persist in fulfilling the Great Commission, the End Times will be a time of great harvesting of lost souls.

And, the End Times could be a time of great victory for Christians, if they are willing to develop their faith to endure hardship.

However, the End Times may not be very comfortable!

~ ~ ~

Again, let me re-emphasize; just because someone has itching ears, and only wants to hear preaching and teaching that is pleasant to the hearing, does not mean they have committed apostasy.

As always, the Lord is the judge. Only he knows when someone has crossed the line. My assignment remains the same – identify those who are vulnerable, and SOUND THE WARNING.

Chapter Eight

Times & Seasons

"Therefore, when they had come together, they asked Him, saying, Lord, will You at this time restore the kingdom to Israel? And He said to them, it is not for you to know times or seasons which the Father has put in His own authority." (Acts 1:6-7).

Pertaining to the sequence of events that precede the second coming of Jesus Christ, theories abound.

Many such theories have progressed to the status of church doctrines, and millions of Christians hold to those doctrines as if they were absolute, unquestionable truth.

This is strange, since Jesus Christ himself plainly responded to his disciples' question about biblical prophecy by saying: *"...IT IS NOT FOR YOU TO KNOW...."*

Some would argue that the response by Jesus applied only to the specific question by his disciples: *"...Lord, will You at this time restore the kingdom to Israel?"*

Actually, his response applies to EVERY TIME OR SEASON, *"...which the Father has put in His own authority."*

This would definitely include the time and season of the return of Jesus Christ, since he himself also said:

"But of that day and hour no one knows, not even the angels in heaven, nor the Son, BUT ONLY THE FATHER." (Mark 13:32).

[AUTHOR'S NOTE: It is likely that Jesus now knows the day and hour of his return. Even though he said: *"...nor the Son..."* one must remember that he was: *"...in the likeness of men..."* (see Philippians 2:5-11). After he was resurrected from the dead, Jesus said: *"...All authority has been given to Me in heaven and on earth."* (Matthew 28:18).]

I have stated in previous writings that I do not know the sequence of End Times events, which, of course, agrees with the previously stated words of Jesus from Acts 1:7:

"...IT IS NOT FOR YOU TO KNOW times or seasons which the Father has put in His own authority."

Regardless, I have heard ministers of the Gospel fervently insist that Jesus will rapture the church (take believers out of the world) at the beginning of a seven-year period known as The Great Tribulation.

Yet, as I examine the scriptures they use to supposedly prove a pre-tribulation rapture, they are inconclusive at best.

I have listened to those who explain that Jesus will return only once; and therefore, the church will remain on the earth during The Great Tribulation.

Others believe the rapture will occur at the middle of The Great Tribulation.

Interestingly, some even question whether there will be a seven-year period identified as The Great Tribulation, citing the fact that believers have experienced great tribulation throughout the history of Christianity.

I have even discussed the End Times with someone who believes sinners are the ones who will be taken out of the world, and we who know the Lord will be left here to reign with Jesus during the Millennium period.

Of course, it's completely understandable that we have many differing opinions about the return of the Lord Jesus, since he himself said: *"...it is not for you to know...."*

But, because of these differing opinions, we have some POTENTIAL PROBLEMS.

What if the sequence of End Time events does not happen exactly as your church is teaching, what then?

I am amazed at ministers of the gospel who display elaborate charts, which neatly categorize, and compartmentalize the events of the End Times, and supposedly show the exact sequence of those events.

What if those events do not happen as we have been told?

What if the sequence of events on the ground does not agree with the sequence of events on the chart?

What if our doctrines eventually turn out to be only theories?

Obviously, a great number of Christians will be confused. Unfortunately, some will be angry with God.

I can just imagine Christians crying out in disappointment: *"I don't understand! Why is this happening? Where is Jesus? He was supposed to take us out of the world before these things happened. This does not agree with my chart!"*

Will Christians be able to adjust if their End Time doctrines prove to be wrong?

I believe the Holy Spirit has impressed upon me that this type of Christian will be vulnerable to apostasy.

As I said earlier, many teachings about the End Times are just theories. Yet, these theories are often taught as absolute truth, and have therefore progressed to the status of church doctrines.

Over the years, these uncertain doctrines have been thoroughly ingrained into people's minds, and they hold fast to them, as if they were as certain as John 3:16.

What if these doctrines fail, as many are sure to do? All of them could not be correct. In light of Jesus' response to his disciples in Acts 1:7, maybe none of them are correct!

How will Christians respond? If they have established the foundation of their faith upon CHURCH DOCTRINES, which are uncertain, will they begin to doubt BIBLE DOCTRINES, which are certain?

You see, all Bible doctrines are definitely certain. For example, listen to the certainty of 1 John 5:13 pertaining to salvation through Jesus Christ:

"These things I have written to you who believe in the name of the Son of God, THAT YOU MAY KNOW that you have eternal life, and that you may continue to believe in the name of the Son of God."

But, all church doctrines are not certain! Some are just theories.

For example, here is a doctrine about the End Times that is definitely a Bible doctrine, rather than a church doctrine, and is therefore certain:

"For the Lord Himself will descend from heaven with a shout, with the voice of an archangel, and with the trumpet of God. And the dead in Christ will rise first. Then we who are alive and remain shall be caught up together with them in the clouds to meet the Lord in the air. And thus we shall always be with the Lord." (1 Thessalonians 4:16-17).

However – BY DIVINE DESIGN – it is not for us to know the day nor the hour, nor the times and seasons, which the Father has put in his own authority. Any attempt to create doctrines beyond what the scriptures actually say, is to create uncertain doctrines!

Probably, some of you are already angry, and complaining: *"You are picking on those who believe in a pre-tribulation rapture."*

Well, I must tell you that I have noticed a certain mentality among many believers who cling to that uncertain doctrine...

"I do not want to hear about hardship! Do not talk to me about persecution, terrorism, tribulation, or apostasy. Soon, maybe today, Jesus will rapture us out of this world, and I will be leaving all this mess behind!

It would be wonderful if the pre-tribulation position were correct, but the truth is, we do not know such things for sure. Therefore, we should not teach them as if they were sure.

Those of us who are teachers of the Bible should be especially careful about what we teach. God's Word admonishes us:

"My brethren, let not many of you become teachers, knowing that we shall receive a stricter judgment." (James 3:1).

Pertaining to the End Times (or, any other time), 1 Thessalonians 5:21 provides us with wise counsel:

"But test and prove all things [until you can recognize] what is good; [to that] hold fast." (AMP).

Therefore, I believe the Spirit of the Lord would have me say to all Christians…

Do not fail to examine, nor be afraid to examine: the doctrines of your church by the standard of God's written Word.

Does the Bible clearly say what you are being taught about the End Times? Or, are those who teach you taking too much liberty with the scriptures, and creating uncertain doctrines?

As we move further into these End Times, deception will not decrease. To the contrary, it will greatly increase.

Apostasy will not *"Flare Up"* for a season, and then fade away. As we draw closer to the return of the Lord, greater and greater animosity will be demonstrated toward Jesus Christ, and toward those who are called by his name.

Increasingly, there will be opportunities for Christians to become offended by the Word of God, and pressured by Satan to depart from the faith.

Therefore, pertaining to the End Times, we must be absolutely certain that…

- **WHAT WE ARE EXPECTING FROM GOD** – is clearly accurate according to his Word.

Otherwise, just leave it in the category of: IT IS NOT FOR ME TO KNOW.

In these last days, many will be deceived, and fall away from the faith. Unfortunately, this will include some who stubbornly believe the End Time doctrines of their church are beyond question, and beyond examination!

Chapter Nine

The End Times Church

"Therefore, come out from among them and be separate, says the Lord. Do not touch what is unclean, and I will receive you. I will be a Father to you, and you shall be My sons and daughters, says the LORD Almighty." (2 Corinthians 6:17-18).

The Holy Spirit has impressed upon me that three types of churches will exist in the End Times...
- THE GODLY CHURCH,
- THE COMPROMISING CHURCH,
- THE APOSTATE CHURCH.

I believe the Lord has also revealed to me that prior to the return of Jesus Christ, one of these churches will disappear! Shall we take a closer look?

The Godly Church

Pastors and members will be conforming to God's Word, and changing to be more like Christ. Look for these characteristics…

CHARACTERISTIC # 1 – Restoration of God-ordained church government:

"And God has appointed these in the church: first apostles, second prophets, third teachers, after that miracles, then gifts of healings, helps, administrations (or, administrators), *varieties of tongues"* (or, intercessors). (1 Corinthians 12:28).

"…He Himself gave some to be apostles, some prophets, some evangelists, and some pastors and teachers." (Ephesians 4:11).

CHARACTERISTIC # 2 – Experiencing the outpouring of the Holy Spirit:

"And it shall come to pass in the last days, says God, that I will pour out of My Spirit on all flesh; your sons and your daughters shall prophesy, your young men shall see visions, your old men shall dream dreams. And on My menservants and on My maidservants I will pour out My Spirit in those days; and they shall prophesy." (Acts 2:17-18).

CHARACTERISTIC # 3 – An emphasis on ingathering of souls, and making disciples of new converts:

"And it shall come to pass in the last days, says God, that I will pour out of My Spirit on all flesh ... and it shall come to pass that whoever calls on the name of the LORD shall be saved." (from Acts 2:17, and verse 21).

"Go therefore and make disciples of all the nations, baptizing them in the name of the Father and of the Son and of the Holy Spirit, teaching them to observe all things that I have commanded you; and lo, I am with you always, even to the end of the age." (Matthew 28:19-20).

CHARACTERISTIC # 4 – Doctrines are based on the integrity of God's Word:

"ALL SCRIPTURE is given by inspiration of God, and is profitable for doctrine, for reproof, for correction, for instruction in righteousness, that the man of God may be complete, thoroughly equipped for every good work." (2 Timothy 3:16-17).

"Forever, O LORD, your word is settled (fixed, set in place) *in heaven. Your faithfulness endures to all generations..."* (Psalm 119:89-90).

CHARACTERISTIC # 5 – Praise and worship are an integral part of the church:

"Praise Him with the sound of the trumpet; praise Him with the lute and harp! Praise Him with the timbrel (tambourine) *and dance; praise Him with stringed instruments and flutes! Praise Him with loud cymbals; praise Him with clashing cymbals! Let everything that has breath praise the LORD. Praise the Lord!"* (Psalm 150:3-6).

CHARACTERISTIC # 6 – Repentance is continuously practiced. Holiness is evident in the lives of the people:

"Therefore, having these promises, beloved (refer to 2 Corinthians 6:16-18), *let us cleanse ourselves from all filthiness of the flesh and spirit, PERFECTING HOLINESS in the fear of God."* (2 Corinthians 7:1).

CHARACTERISTIC # 7 – The restoration of Israel will be recognized, as foretold by the prophets. The Godly church will stand with Israel in the last days:

"And so all Israel will be saved, as it is written: the Deliverer will come out of Zion, and He will turn away ungodliness from Jacob; for this is My covenant with them, when I take away their sins." (Romans 11:26-27).

The Compromising Church

The compromising church will have weak leadership. The pastors may know the truth of God's Word, but they are afraid to declare it, lest someone be offended. Watch for these identifying characteristics...

CHARACTERISTIC # 1 – Tolerance will become the chief doctrine – tolerance of sin, and tolerance of other religions. Absolutes will be looked upon as a lack of love.

"It is actually reported that there is sexual immorality among you, and of a kind that does not occur even among pagans: A man has his father's wife. And you are proud! Shouldn't you rather have been filled with grief and have put out of your fellowship the man who did this?" (1 Corinthians 5:1-2 NIV).

"For if he who comes preaches another Jesus whom we have not preached, or if you receive a different spirit which you have not received, or a different gospel which you have not accepted – you may well put up with it!" (2 Corinthians 11:4).

"You shall have no other gods before Me." (Exodus 20:2).

CHARACTERISTIC # 2 – The people will become selective in what they are willing to hear from the Bible. They will especially turn away from words of correction:

"For the time will come when they will not endure sound doctrine, but according to their own desires, because they have itching ears, (ears that want to be tickled) *they will heap up for themselves teachers; and they will turn their ears away from the truth, and be turned aside to fables."* (2 Timothy 4:3-4).

CHARACTERISTIC # 3 – The traditions of man, and human philosophy will replace the truth of God's Word:

"Beware lest anyone cheat you through philosophy and empty deceit, according to the tradition of men, according to the basic principles of the world, and not according to Christ." (Colossians 2:8).

"Making the word of God of no effect (deprived of authority) *THROUGH YOUR TRADITION which you have handed down. And many such things you do."* (Mark 7:13).

CHARACTERISTIC # 4 – The people will view sin lightly, and become less and less serious about godliness. They will see no need for repentance in their lives:

"But immorality (sexual vice) and all impurity [of lustful, rich, wasteful living] or greediness must not even be named among you, as is fitting and proper among saints (God's consecrated people). Let there be no filthiness (obscenity, indecency) nor foolish and sinful (silly and corrupt) talk, nor coarse jesting, which are not fitting or becoming; but instead voice your thankfulness [to God]." (Ephesians 5:3-4 AMP).

CHARACTERISTIC # 5 – The authority of leadership will be challenged and opposed. Those described as GRIEVOUS WOLVES will come in among the people, and exercise control over the pastor, and in some cases, replace the pastor:

"For I know this, that after my departing shall grievous wolves enter in among you, not sparing the flock. Also of your own selves shall men arise, speaking perverse things, to draw away disciples after them." (Acts 20:29-30 KJV).

"…I have this against you: YOU TOLERATE that woman Jezebel, who calls herself a prophetess. By her teaching she misleads MY SERVANTS into sexual immorality and the eating of food sacrificed to idols. I have given her time to repent of her immorality, but she is unwilling." (Revelation 2:20-21 NIV).

The Apostate Church

As the return of Christ draws nearer, the apostate church will become more visible. Its numbers will be swelled by those who are departing from the faith. Strangely, those in the apostate church will be convinced that they are in the true church! Be vigilant, and watch for these characteristics...

CHARACTERISTIC # 1 – The people will listen to deceiving spirits, rather than God's Holy Spirit. Consequently, their beliefs will degrade into doctrines of demons:

"Now the Spirit expressly (clearly) *says that in latter times some will depart from the faith, giving heed to deceiving* (seducing) *spirits and doctrines of demons."* (1 Timothy 4:1).

CHARACTERISTIC # 2 – The redemptive work of Jesus Christ will be explained away, demoted, and eventually denied:

"...certain men whose condemnation was written about long ago have secretly slipped in among you. They are godless men, who change the grace of our God into a license for immorality and deny Jesus Christ our only Sovereign and Lord." (Jude 4 NIV).

CHARACTERISTIC # 3 – The truth of God's Word will be exchanged for lies. Lies that cleverly erode the truth, and strip away the authority of the Bible:

"They exchanged the truth of God for a lie, and worshiped and served created things rather than the Creator – who is forever praised." (Romans 1:25 NIV).

CHARACTERISTIC # 4 – The people will not be able to distinguish between good and evil. Sin will be explained away, or justified, and eventually, just outright accepted:

"Woe to those who call evil good, and good evil; who put darkness for light, and light for darkness; who put bitter for sweet, and sweet for bitter!" (Isaiah 5:20).

CHARACTERISTIC # 5 – Pastors and church members alike will be filled with gross sexual immorality (lasciviousness – the absence of restraint). Those who pervert God's laws of nature (homosexuals, bisexuals, transvestites, and concubines) will fill the pews and pulpits:

"Therefore God also gave them up to uncleanness, in the lusts of their hearts, to dishonor their bodies among themselves." (Romans 1:24).

CHARACTERISTIC # 6 – Church leaders and church members will be given over to a debased (reprobate, depraved) mind:

"And even as they did not like to retain God in their knowledge, God gave them over to a debased mind, to do those things which are not fitting." (Romans 1:28).

~ ~ ~

Perhaps you can think of other identifying characteristics for each type of church, but listen carefully to a word from the Holy Spirit, and the primary purpose for this chapter…

As we draw closer to the return of the Lord, the lines of separation between the godly and the ungodly will become more and more clearly defined. As a result, the day will come when THE COMPROMISING CHURCH WILL DISAPPEAR.

Some will get serious with God, and move up to The Godly Church.

Many will refuse to repent of compromise. They will become increasingly angry about the intolerance of God's Word, and become rebellious toward God. Sadly, they will end up in The Apostate Church.

You must decide – in which of these churches will you reside?

Chapter Ten

The Severity of Apostasy

"For IT IS IMPOSSIBLE for those who were once enlightened, and have tasted the heavenly gift, and have become partakers of the Holy Spirit, and have tasted the good word of God and the powers of the age to come, if they fall away, to renew them again to repentance, since they crucify again for themselves the Son of God, and put Him to an open shame." (Hebrews 6:4-6).

In certain churches, the Sunday sermons seem to imply that one could be repeatedly lost and saved, depending upon their weekly performance. Usually, such preaching fails to distinguish between RELATIONSHIP with God, and FELLOWSHIP with God.

We enter into RELATIONSHIP with God by accepting Jesus Christ as our Savior, and by trusting in the blood Jesus shed upon the cross for the forgiveness and cleansing of our sins:

"In Him we have redemption through His blood, the forgiveness of sins, according to the riches of His grace." (Ephesians 1:7).

After entering into relationship with God, FELLOWSHIP is maintained by continuously confessing to God, the sins we commit after accepting Jesus as Savior:

"...if we walk in the light as He is in the light, we have FELLOWSHIP WITH ONE ANOTHER (fellowship between God and man), *and the blood of Jesus Christ His Son cleanses us from all sin. If we say that we have no sin, we deceive ourselves, and the truth is not in us. If we confess our sins, He is faithful and just to forgive us our sins and to cleanse us from all unrighteousness."* (1 John 1:7-9).

After we have accepted Jesus Christ, sin breaks our fellowship with God, but not our relationship. Even when we sin, we are still God's children, and he is still our Heavenly Father. Once we confess our sins to God, our fellowship is restored.

Apostasy, on the other hand, severs the relationship between God and man, and after apostasy has been committed, there is no such thing as getting saved again!

Apostasy is a condition from which there is no return. Our opening scriptures say of someone who has committed apostasy:

"...IT IS IMPOSSIBLE ... TO RENEW THEM AGAIN TO REPENTANCE...."

Of course, the cause of apostasy is sin; but specifically, the failure to deal with sin, or the failure to maintain fellowship with God.

Be aware that sin is not limited to sexual immorality or greed. Anything that influences a person to turn back and stop following God is sin! In these End Times, some will turn away from God, simply because he does not meet their personal expectations.

Regardless, the person who fails to deal with sin will eventually become hardened to sin, and will no longer respond to conviction from the Holy Spirit, or conviction from the Word of God. In time, such hardness could cause a person to decide that they no longer believe in Jesus Christ.

It is this DENIAL OF JESUS CHRIST that causes one to cross the line, and enter into the state of apostasy.

A Contrast of Denials

The denial of Jesus Christ that leads to apostasy is obviously more serious than the denial by Peter when Jesus was arrested in the Garden of Gethsemane.

Peter temporarily denied that he knew the Lord Jesus because of FEAR, not because he rejected the Lord.

The denial of Jesus that leads to apostasy is a REJECTION of the redemptive work of the Lord Jesus; specifically, a rejection of his shed blood for the remission of sins.

~ ~ ~

The book of Hebrews provides us with an example of apostasy, or at least a warning about the possibility of apostasy.

Although many of the spiritual principles in the book of Hebrews apply to all believers, we must keep in mind that the epistle was initially written to Jews, and more specifically to believing Jews – those who had accepted Jesus Christ as Messiah.

A careful reading of Hebrews, chapter 10, reveals that God was warning believing Jews not to turn back to Judaism. Likely, the Holy Spirit was also describing what had already happened to certain Jews who had returned to Judaism, and thus, committed apostasy.

Throughout the New Testament, we read of the enormous pressure that was upon the Jews to reject Jesus as the Christ – pressure from the Jewish religious leaders, pressure from Jewish culture, and pressure from their own families and relatives.

Equally so, there was enormous pressure upon believing Jews to abandon their faith in Jesus, and return to Judaism; pressure that frequently included death as the alternative!

Listen to a portion of Hebrews 10, as the Holy Spirit warns believing Jews of apostasy, a fate worse than death:

"For if we (believing Jews) *sin willfully after we have received the knowledge of the truth, there no longer remains a sacrifice for sins, but a certain fearful expectation of judgment, and fiery indignation which will devour the adversaries. Anyone who has rejected Moses' law dies without mercy on the testimony of two or three witnesses. Of how much worse punishment, do you suppose, will he be thought worthy who has trampled the Son of God underfoot, counted the blood of the covenant by which he was sanctified a common* (or unholy) *thing, and insulted the Spirit of grace?"* (verses 26-29).

On the following page, I have separated the above scriptures into individual phrases, and added my explanatory notes.

"For if we sin willfully after we have received the knowledge of the truth…"
- After a Jew receives the knowledge of the truth, and understands that Jesus is the Christ, and the only way to God, returning to Judaism would be a willful, blatant, deliberate sin.

"…there no longer remains A SACRIFICE FOR SINS."
- After you receive the sacrifice of Jesus for the remission of sins, you cannot go back to offering animal sacrifices.

"Anyone who has rejected Moses' law dies without mercy on the testimony of two or three witnesses."
- Referring to unbelieving, or disobedient Jews under the Old Covenant.

"Of how much WORSE PUNISHMENT, do you suppose, will he be thought worthy who has trampled the Son of God underfoot, counted the blood of the covenant by which HE WAS SANCTIFIED a common thing, and insulted the Spirit of grace?"
- Referring to believing Jews under the New Covenant. Please take note – the Word of God identifies such Jews as those who WERE SANCTIFIED by the blood of Jesus.

As previously stated, it is the rejection of the REDEMPTIVE WORK of Jesus Christ, by someone who had previously accepted it, that leads to apostasy.

From Hebrews 10:29, please notice again the rebellion evident in those Jews who were once believers, but now apostate…

1) Trampled the Son of God underfoot.
2) Counted the blood of the covenant (the blood of Jesus Christ) by which they were sanctified, a common, unholy thing.
3) Insulted the Spirit of grace.

Be aware that such rebellion would also apply to Gentiles, who accept Jesus Christ, but later turn away from the truth.

And, the punishment is SEVERE…

"…IT IS IMPOSSIBLE … TO RENEW THEM AGAIN TO REPENTANCE…."

Be on guard; seducing, deceiving spirits are rising up in these End Times, trying to convince Christians to embrace doctrines of demons. Do not allow yourself to…

1) View sin lightly.
2) Become offended by God's Word.
3) Question the integrity of God's Word.
4) Become ashamed of Jesus Christ.
5) Become rebellious toward God.

Jesus warned us about these End Times:

"At that time many will TURN AWAY from the faith (become offended) *and will betray and hate each other."* (Matthew 24:10 NIV).

The same verse from the Amplified Bible reads as follows:

"And then many will be offended and repelled and begin to distrust and desert [Him whom they ought to trust and obey], and will stumble and fall away, and betray one another, and pursue one another with hatred."

The Lord knows the beginning to the end. It was he who stirred up the apostles' hearts, and inspired them to pen the scriptures, and warn us about The Great Apostasy.

And, although my written words do not bear the weight of God's written Word; yet, it was God who likewise stirred up my heart to warn his people about The Great Apostasy.

God loves his children, and does not want to lose any of them!

Chapter Eleven

The Way of Repentance

"Even though we speak like this, dear friends, (severe warnings about apostasy), *we are confident of better things in your case – things that accompany salvation."* (Hebrews 6:9 NIV).

"But our way is not that of those who draw back to eternal misery (perdition) and are utterly destroyed, but we are of those who believe – who cleave to and trust in and rely on God through Jesus Christ, the Messiah – and by faith preserve the soul." (Hebrews 10:39 AMP).

In the last chapter, we learned that once someone commits apostasy, it is impossible to renew them again to repentance.

Repentance then, is the KEY to avoiding apostasy! But, the question is, do we really understand repentance?

[BIBLE DEFINITION: Repentance – To change one's mind, or to change one's purpose. A reversal of decision, always involving a change for the better. Repentance involves both a turning from sin, and a turning to God.]

Repentance is not just saying: *"I'm sorry!"* For too long, we have overlooked a key statement by John the Baptist:

"But when he saw many of the Pharisees and Sadducees coming to his baptism, he said to them, Brood of vipers! Who warned you to flee from the wrath to come? Therefore BEAR FRUITS WORTHY OF REPENTANCE." (Matthew 3:7-8).

The repentance John the Baptist spoke of was preparing the way for people to receive the coming Messiah. In this chapter, we are focusing upon repentance that continues to take place in a believer's life after they have received Jesus. Yet, the characteristics of repentance are the same.

Listen again to the last part of the above scriptures: *"...Therefore bear fruits WORTHY of repentance."*

Repentance must be WORTHWHILE, not WORTHLESS! Listen again to Matthew 3:8 from the Amplified Bible: *"Bring forth fruit that is consistent with repentance – let your lives prove your change of heart."*

Plainly speaking, repentance is not just WORDS, but rather, genuine repentance will be demonstrated by ACTIONS.

Allow me to explain, and let us begin with the basics – SALVATION. When we accept salvation through Jesus Christ, we do so by accepting A FREE GIFT of God's grace:

"For by grace (unmerited favor from God) *you have been saved through faith, and that not of yourselves; it is THE GIFT OF GOD, not of works, lest anyone should boast."* (Ephesians 2:8-9).

Yet, in order to receive the free gift, one must repent. All who come to God must turn from THEIR OWN WAY – to Jesus Christ – who is THE WAY TO GOD:

"All we like sheep have gone astray; we have turned, every one, TO HIS OWN WAY; and the LORD has laid on Him the iniquity of us all." (Isaiah 53:6).

"Jesus said ... I AM THE WAY, the truth, and the life. No one comes to the Father except through Me." (John 14:6).

The true test for judging if repentance for salvation has occurred is actions (a changed life), not just words:

"Therefore, if anyone is in Christ, he is a new creation; old things have passed away; behold, all things have become new." (2 Corinthians 5:17).

Similarly, after salvation, repentance must continue to involve ACTIONS, more so than just WORDS!

Those who enter into sin, and afterwards declare, *"I REPENT,"* should also show forth fruits of repentance by...

1) Apologizing to everyone to whom an apology is due, and do so in public if necessary.
2) Actively seeking forgiveness from ALL who have been touched by their sin.
3) Striving to be reconciled to those they have violated, rather than leaving a trail of burned bridges behind them.
4) Submitting themselves to the discipline of godly peers; specifically, those who stand in a position of higher spiritual authority.
5) Willingly stepping aside from ministry for a season, if spiritual discipline so dictates, until fruits of repentance can be observed.

Without bearing fruit that is WORTHY of repentance – showing forth results that are worthwhile, rather than worthless – how can we know if true repentance has taken place?

These are dangerous times; sin abounds, and is readily accessible. But, God is also at work, cleaning up his children, and rescuing them from the paths of apostasy.

But, God's people must also do their part, and stop resisting the Holy Spirit…

- It is time to quit living in deliberate sin, and trying to hide behind a once saved, always saved doctrine.
- It is time to dismantle secret lives, and secret agendas, and begin to walk in the light.
- It is time to hold on, not just to faith, but also to a good conscience, and thereby avoid shipwrecked faith.
- It is time to become honest before a holy God, and allow the FEAR OF THE LORD to be restored in our lives.

"For the time has come for judgment to begin at the house of God; and if it begins with us first, what will be the end of those who do not obey the gospel of God? Now if the righteous one is scarcely saved, where will the ungodly and the sinner appear?" (1 Peter 4:17-18).

Following is a prayer of repentance, for those who are serious about dealing with sin in their lives…

A Prayer of Repentance

Heavenly Father, I come to you in the name of Jesus Christ.
I come to you in honesty, confessing that I have sinned, and admitting that I have not genuinely repented.
I cry out to you, Lord; please help me! I need the power of your Holy Spirit to help me truly repent, and to set me free from the bondage of sin.
I desire to show forth genuine fruits of repentance. With your help, Lord, I turn away from sin, and I turn wholly to you.
I acknowledge anew, that you, Lord Jesus, by your sacrifice on the cross, and by your shed blood, have made available to me, a right standing before God.
I acknowledge again, my faith in your saving grace, and I declare afresh: Jesus Christ, you are my Lord, my Savior, my God, in whom I will trust.
Amen.

Epilogue

In the course of writing this book, I was attacked by a harassing evil spirit, which was assaulting my mind with doubts pertaining to the truth and integrity of God's Word.

At first, I did not recognize the attack as an evil spirit, but as I prayed, the Holy Spirit revealed to me that I was being attacked by A SPIRIT OF UNBELIEF.

I wondered why this particular spirit was attacking my mind? I accepted Jesus Christ a long time ago, and made the decision to believe the Word of God (the Bible) is absolute truth. Regardless, this demon bombarded my mind with doubt for many days.

Repeatedly, in order to combat this evil spirit, I expressed my faith in God. I looked up into Heaven, and declared...

- I believe you are God,
- I believe your Word is truth,
- Lord Jesus, I believe you shed your blood for the remission of my sins,
- I believe you are faithful to watch over your Word, and fulfill it in the lives of those who trust in you!

Obviously, one purpose for the attack was to discourage me from completing this book. Satan does not want Christians to be aware of the dangers of apostasy.

Actually, I thought the book was finished, but the Lord prompted me to write this final section to warn his people about this spirit of unbelief.

~ ~ ~

Increasingly, in these End Times, this evil spirit will be rising up to challenge the truth and integrity of the Bible by attacking God's people with doubt.

Sometimes, the attack will be DIRECTLY against our minds in the form of arguments, (reasoning, or imaginations), as this spirit exalts itself against the knowledge of God:

"For the weapons of our warfare are not carnal but mighty in God for pulling down strongholds, casting down arguments and every high thing that exalts itself against the knowledge of God, bringing every thought into captivity to the obedience of Christ."

As the above verses instruct us, we must cast down these imaginations, replace them with the truth of God's Word, and bring every thought of doubt or unbelief into captivity to the obedience of Christ.

At other times, this spirit of unbelief will attack us INDIRECTLY through the words and actions of other people. 2 Peter 3:3-4 warns us about such people:

"Knowing this first: that scoffers will come in the last days, walking according to their own lusts, and saying, Where is the promise of His coming? For since the fathers fell asleep, all things continue as they were from the beginning of creation."

These scoffers (or mockers) will challenge the integrity of God's Word by planting seeds of doubt: *"…Where is the promise of His coming?"*

If Christians are not on guard, they could look around at the moral decline of society, and wonder: *"Why hasn't the Lord returned? Is he going to return, or is the Bible just a big fairy tale?"*

Again, such imaginations must be cast down, and replaced with the truth of God's Word. Hebrews 10:37-39 both instructs us, and warns us:

"For yet a little while, and He who is coming will come and will not tarry. Now the just shall live by faith; but if anyone draws back, My soul has no pleasure in him. But we are not of those who draw back to perdition, but of those who believe to the saving of the soul."

In the early chapters, we discovered that some will fall away from the faith, because they refuse to deal with sin, whether overt or covert, and will enter into apostasy.

In the middle chapters, we discussed the fact that some will fall away from the faith, because they are disappointed with God. He has not met their personal expectations, or his Word disagrees with their values.

Now, in these closing pages, I am warning you to be alert, and on guard against the spirit of unbelief, who will come to challenge the truth and integrity of God's Word, and pressure your mind with doubt.

And, be ever aware that the intentions of these demons of doubt are to lead you into the paths of apostasy!

At the beginning of his short epistle, Jude said he intended to write about salvation, but instead, found it necessary to write about another subject:

"Dear friends, although I was very eager to write to you about the salvation we share, I felt I had to write and urge you TO CONTEND FOR THE FAITH that was once for all entrusted to the saints." (Jude 3 NIV).

[BIBLE DEFINITION: Contend – To struggle for, as a combatant.]

Many Christians do not like to hear such words. Regardless, there is a fight involved in maintaining our faith!

The writer of the book of Hebrews sums up the matter, and gives us one last warning about apostasy:

"Therefore we must give the more earnest heed to the things we have heard, lest we drift away." (Hebrews 2:1).

The KJV says it in this manner:

"Therefore we ought to give the more earnest heed to the things which we have heard, lest at any time we should let them slip."

Using a combination of the two versions, I conclude…

More than ever before, we must pay close attention to the truth we have heard from God's Word, lest at any time, or in any way, we could let the truth slip, and we drift away!

Notes

Jack Michael Outreach Ministries Ministry Newsletter

Most months, depending on outreach schedules and operational priorities, Jack Michael Outreach Ministries publishes a ministry newsletter.

Jack Michael is a FOUNDATION BUILDER. As such, you will quickly recognize from the newsletter that he is committed to building a strong foundation of God's Word into the lives of God's people.

Jack Michael has been given the God-ordained assignment as a WATCHMAN ON THE WALLS in the body of Christ. As such, via the newsletter, he often deals with controversial issues that affect the body of Christ, and frequently warns God's people of existing and impending deception.

The ministry newsletter is brief, straightforward, and easily readable. It is available, free of charge, to God's people living in the United States, and also foreign countries.

For those who desire to receive the newsletter, PLEASE REQUEST IT. Send your clearly printed name/address to Jack Michael Outreach Ministries. You may use the coupon at the end of this book.

Other Books by Jack Michael

Deception In The End Times   (retail $7.00)

"What will be the sign of your coming, and of the end of the age?" When the disciples asked Jesus this question, his immediate response revealed a subject area that is seldom mentioned by end time prophecy teachers.

"And Jesus answered and said to them: Take heed that no one deceives you!"

I am convinced that DECEPTION, at an accelerated pace, will be the primary sign pointing to the return of Christ. And, much of that deception will be aimed directly at the church.

It is with these thoughts in mind, that I present to you, A COMMON SENSE HANDBOOK FOR DISCERNING THE SIGNS OF THE TIMES.

The Best Way To Know God's Will   (retail) $5.00

Have you ever had wishful thoughts that God would leave Heaven for a little while, come down to earth, lead us about by the hand, and show us his will firsthand?

If so, there is good news for you in this book! God did leave Heaven for a little while. He came down to earth, people followed him about, and he showed them the will of God firsthand. HIS NAME WAS JESUS.

The Christ Conspiracy (Novel)   (retail) $10.00

What kind of child could potentially grow up to become a dangerous cult leader?

What would be the factors that propel his life toward inevitable destruction?

In *"The Christ Conspiracy,"* Jack Michael unfolds the uncanny rise and fall of a fictitious cult leader, and the decisions, ranging from the logical to the bizarre, that govern the ascent and descent.

Will God Supply All Your Needs?   (retail) $5.00

Philippians 4:19 is one of the most familiar, and one of the most claimed verses of scripture in the Bible!
"And my God shall supply all your need according to His riches in glory by Christ Jesus."
However, like other promises of God, there are some things we must FIRST do in order to qualify to receive the promise!

Foundation Building
(A Study Guide For Christians)   (retail) $12.00

(A spiral-bound notebook containing 20 lessons designed to build a strong foundation of God's word into the lives of Christians, especially new Christians).

Jesus said: *"Therefore everyone who hears these words of mine and puts them into practice is like a wise man who built his house on the rock. The rain came down, the streams rose, and the winds blew and beat against that house; yet it did not fall, because it had its FOUNDATION on the rock."* (Matthew 7:24-25 NIV).

It is essential for every born-again Christian to have a strong, biblical foundation of God's word in their life. This is especially true during these tumultuous last days, because DECEPTION IS ABOUNDING, and will be ever increasing as we progress further into the End Times. When properly employed, this FOUNDATION BUILDING study course will help provide that strong foundation.

Whether you are the teacher or pupil, I challenge you as the Apostle Paul once challenged his spiritual son, Timothy: *"Be DILIGENT to present yourself approved to God, a worker who does not need to be ashamed, RIGHTLY DIVIDING* (rightly handling, accurately analyzing, skillfully teaching) *the word of truth."* (2 Timothy 2:15).

Grievous Wolves (Hindering spirits that Challenge and Oppose Spiritual Leadership) (retail $6.00)

Satan fully intends to destroy the church of the Lord Jesus Christ. Now, perhaps you are thinking, *"Yes, those are his intentions, but he cannot do it, because the Bible says Jesus will build his church, and the gates of hell will not prevail against it."*

This is true. On the authority of the scriptures, Satan cannot destroy the church of Jesus Christ AS A WHOLE.

However, it is also an unfortunate truth that Satan and his agents have succeeded in destroying individual churches within the body of Christ.

One of the destructive forces that Satan has employed down through the ages is described by the Apostle Paul as GRIEVOUS WOLVES.

Why Haven't My Loved Ones Accepted Jesus Christ? (retail) $6.00

"Very rarely will anyone die for a righteous man, though for a good man someone might possibly dare to die. But God demonstrates his own love for us in this: While we were still sinners, Christ died for us. Since we have now been justified by his blood, how much more shall we be saved from God's wrath through him!" (Romans 5:7-9 NIV).

With God's love and mercy leaping from the pages of the Bible through the above verses, and multiple other verses in the New Testament, one has to wonder why the world is not racing to accept Jesus Christ as their Lord and Savior?

How could anyone not desire forgiveness and cleansing of sin, and deliverance from the wrath of God? Why would anyone not desire to be clothed with the righteousness of God? How could anyone not desire to walk in harmony and fellowship with their creator?

It often seems like a great mystery, but actually, the Bible provides us with very clear answers as to why much of the world refuses to accept Jesus Christ.

Saving The Children (retail $8.00)

The heart of Jesus still cries out: *"...Let the little children come to me, and do not hinder them, for the kingdom of God belongs to such as these."* (Mark 10:14).

The warning of Jesus still resounds: *"...Whoever causes one of these little ones who believe in Me to sin, it would be better for him if a millstone were hung around his neck, and he were drowned in the depth of the sea."* (Matthew 18:6).

There is a fierce battle raging in these End Times; a spiritual battle for the souls of the children. On the one hand, God is pouring out his Holy Spirit upon the children and young people. On the other hand, Satan is trying to destroy the souls of the children.

In the middle are the parents. These are the days for SERIOUS CHRISTIAN PARENTING.

To order books, or request the ministry newsletter, clip or copy the below order blank, enclose payment for books, and send to:

Jack Michael Outreach Ministries
PO Box 117
Clemmons, NC 27012

No postage is required for retail, domestic orders within the United States.

For wholesale orders, please contact Jack Michael Outreach Ministries at the above address.

Quantity	Title	Price
_____	_____	_____
_____	_____	_____
_____	_____	_____
_____	_____	_____

TOTAL ENCLOSED $_____

Name _____

Address _____

City _____ State _____

Zip Code _____

1956 - 2036
  80
─────
2036